THE QUIET REVOLUTION

The Quiet Revolution

The Radical Impact of Jesus on Men of His Time

by James D. Smart

The Westminster Press
Philadelphia

STANDARD BOOK NO. 664–24867–5

LIBRARY OF CONGRESS CATALOG CARD NO. 69–20340

BS
2430
.S57

PUBLISHED BY THE WESTMINSTER PRESS ®
Philadelphia, Pennsylvania

PRINTED IN THE UNITED STATES OF AMERICA

CONTENTS

INTRODUCTION: JESUS REMEMBERED
IN HUMAN ENCOUNTER

THE ENCOUNTERS AND DIALOGUES of Jesus with representative persons have been constant companions of my ministry from its very beginning and they have grown in their significance for me with the years. Their interest at first was the opportunity they offered to let the Biblical text come alive for a congregation by using the resources of scholarship and a disciplined imagination to reconstruct from the meager text a series of scenes in which Jesus stood over against men of his time in sharp contrast and expressed his mind in relation to them with a radical decisiveness. In each instance the outcome of the exposition was intended to be self-identification of the modern man with the individual in the story and a consequent encounter with the mind and spirit of Jesus. Only gradually did I begin to see that this was the very purpose which the stories served in the traditions and preaching of the early church, each of the individuals encountered having clearly a representative character that facilitated the hearer's process of self-identification.

In my reading I became aware very early that in several instances I had come upon an interpretation of the passage which differed considerably from any that had been heretofore offered. In 1935 no one seemed to have noticed that a number of Jesus' parables were directly in line with the prophetic parable in the Old Testament and, far from being any mere illustration or exposition of a spiritual truth, were actually a prophetic device to cut through the blindness of a man and lay him open to God. In

September, 1936, I published in the *Expository Times* a study[1] of the parable of the good Samaritan, making use of this insight. One feature of that interpretation was, in contrast to the dominant view which separated the parable from its context, the discovery that the parable, understood in its prophetic character, becomes an essential part of Jesus' dialogue with the religious lawyer, and, moreover, that Jesus deals rather roughly with him in his arrogance and obtuseness. In short, the dialogue began to take on a new significance as an example of Jesus' pastoral approach, of Jesus' way of dealing with problem people.

This insight, in turn, provided a new approach to the difficult and consistently embarrassing story of Jesus and the Canaanite woman. Just as Jesus led the lawyer on to make something of a fool of himself in answering his own question, so Jesus in this rare encounter with a foreign woman led his disciples on to expose their crude prejudices against foreigners. Also, here the two-edged character of many of Jesus' words began to appear more clearly: that they cut two ways at once, being words of judgment upon one hearer and at the same time words of grace to another, binding one man and loosing the other. The encounter with Simon and the woman from the street is the most vivid example of this two-edged sword, but, once it is recognized as characteristic of Jesus' way of dealing with people, one begins to see it in many of his words. In July, 1939, I published a study[2] of Jesus and the Canaanite woman in the *Expository Times,* suggesting as an explanation of Jesus' seemingly harsh words that in this one situation he was dealing not just with a foreign woman but also with a serious problem of nationalistic prejudice in his disciples.

None of the other eight studies has been published but each has been worked over many times in lectures and in sermons, and with each reworking I have become more conscious of a consistent representation of Jesus' person which appears in all of them, no matter which strand of the church's tradition they stem from. The Jesus whose distinctive mission stands out in contrast to that of John the Baptist, the Jesus who goes to dinner with Levi and his fellow tax collectors, the Jesus who has dinner with Simon, and the Jesus who can do nothing to save either Judas or himself from their tragic ends is the same Jesus who meets Paul on the Damascus road and demands to know how in the service of God he can be his enemy. These stories are distillations of the church's memory of what it was like to be confronted by Jesus, but, as the story of Paul's conversion shows, the church made no distinction between confrontation with Jesus in the flesh and confrontation with him as the risen Lord. Both in the flesh and in the Spirit the encounter with him brought a man's whole life under the judgment of God and laid open the possibility of a new life in the strength of God's forgiveness and grace. Therefore, as the debate concerning the Jesus of history and the Christ of faith began afresh, it seemed to me that these stories had a contribution to make. They provide no material for the writing of a biography, but they do bring vividly before us a person, a human mind and spirit, that is not likely to be confused with anyone else in history, and they depict him not in lonely isolation but involved in the problems of other persons' lives, doing a work that was the fulfillment of his destiny.

The stories warn us in every instance, however, how hidden the Christ of faith was in the Jesus of history. John the Baptist, with all his prophetic insight, remained uncertain what to make of Jesus. Again and again, men who were most deeply versed in Scripture were blind to the work of God which was reality before their very eyes. Paul, passionately devoted to the God of Israel, saw at first in Jesus not the fulfillment of Israel's destiny but, rather, the destruction of all that the centuries of Israel's faith had built up. Judas, one of the Twelve, who had companied with Jesus for months and had shared his mission in some degree, was still so blind to him that he sent him to his death. Even Peter, the disciple who was closest to Jesus, did not really grasp the dimensions of the adventure on which he was embarked or the depth of the mystery that was embodied in the person and vocation of Jesus. The ultimate reality of this person was hidden until it was revealed in his resurrection, and yet in its hiddenness it was present in his historical encounters with men, determining the character of the encounter and pressing to break through the

blindness of men and achieve its purpose. Therefore, the church
did not find it sufficient to remember only the risen Lord, who in
detachment from the Jesus of history might well have become
just one of the many lords of Hellenistic religion. They remembered the Lord *Jesus* with a human face and a human mind
and they remembered the human words with which he brought
men into immediate confrontation with God's judgment and
grace. Their whole relation with God was mediated by this
human person whom they could never again forget.

The work of the form critics and particularly of Bultmann
has put an end to all naïve reconstructing of a biography of Jesus
from the Gospels. Even those scholars who have been most
active in renewing the quest for the historical Jesus have no intention of encouraging a return to such naïveté. Rather, their
concern is to show that when criticism has finished its task, there
is still solid evidence of a distinctive historical person named
Jesus and that the church's memory of Jesus' words and actions
is inseparable from its memory of his continued presence with
his people as their risen Lord. But radical skepticism about the
possibility of attributing anything in the Gospels directly to Jesus
such as Bultmann expressed in *Jesus and the Word,* since form
criticism could never be sure whether the origin was with Jesus
himself or in the earliest stage of the tradition, had serious consequences. For Bultmann himself and for many others, it meant
the removal of Jesus' *person* from its central place in the Christian faith, the kerygma of the church becoming the focal point
of God's action. But more generally it has operated as a restraint
that has made men, in their desire to leave naïveté behind, timid
and uncertain in their presentation of the Jesus of the Gospels.

This skepticism and the timidity which issues from it has gone
much too far and needs to be counteracted. In the Old Testament there is frequently a mingling of legend and history, particularly in the representation of prophets in the historical books,
but we do not let this prevent us from recovering a fair estimate
of the historical figure of a prophet such as Elijah. The Book
of Jeremiah came into its present form after passing through the
hands of Baruch and a number of other editors, but we would

never despair of recovering the essential character of Jeremiah's person and mission. Why, then, should there be this radical skepticism in relation to the gospel records which continue the Old Testament tradition of retaining the memory of men in whom God's work of judgment and grace was carried forward? Certainly allowance has to be made for the remolding of the tradition in its transmission. But the person and mission of Jesus stand out with a distinctiveness that surely cannot be obscured any more than they can be in the instance of Isaiah or Jeremiah. These ten studies of how the church remembered Jesus in different kinds of encounter are offered in the hope that they may encourage a fresh confidence in the validity and integrity of the early church's memory.

The title requires perhaps a word of explanation. When we take seriously that these encounters represent the church's memory of the impact of Jesus upon men and upon established attitudes of his time, we begin to realize how revolutionary Jesus and his gospel were and how natural it was that men who cherished the established order should want him silenced. Not only was he propagating an order of life which set in question the foundation principles of a God-fearing society, firmly anchored in an infallible Scripture, but, even more seriously, he was shaking men at the point of their inmost security, concerning the basis on which they counted themselves acceptable to God. God's ruthless claim on man came to expression in Jesus in such a radical way that it must have seemed to make valueless and innocuous all the assurances of the long-established religious authorities. He could not offer to men the freedom and blessing of an unconditional openness to God without claiming from them an equally unconditional binding of their wills to the will of God. The consequent tension with the existing order must have been explosive. It disturbed even such prophetically-minded people as the followers of John the Baptist.

And yet this revolutionary character of Jesus and his gospel is frequently concealed from the minds of Bible-reading Christians. Because his revolution was a quiet revolution, with no loud public protests, with no program for the reform of existing religious institutions, with no strategy for the seizure of power, it is possible to miss the radical quality that was inherent in every part of it and to picture Jesus' ministry as such a gentle, peaceful religious program that not even the most conservative religionist could be disturbed by it. So also those who think loud public protests and strategies for the seizure of power are essential for any effective Christian revolution may be deceived by the quietness of Jesus' approach into underestimating the subversive quality of his mission. It may, therefore, be instructive for us in the midst of present demands for radical change both in the church and in society to look into this series of encounters of Jesus with representative persons and to ask ourselves what it was in him and his gospel that constituted a revolutionary force capable of turning the world upside down.

Chapter I

JESUS AND JOHN THE BAPTIST

THERE IS NO BETTER EXAMPLE in the Gospels of how Jesus was remembered in an encounter, the memory being overlaid with later traditions and yet being clearly distinguishable in spite of them, than the record of Jesus' relation with John the Baptist. The only immediate encounter of Jesus with John of which we have record took place just before John's mission was brought to an abrupt close by his arrest and imprisonment and before Jesus' own mission began. The Fourth Gospel portrays the two missions as proceeding parallel for a time but it makes no suggestion that the two men ever met again. The variation from the Synoptic account is most likely due to a recollection that a John the Baptist mission was still being carried on by his disciples during Jesus' ministry.

That Jesus was baptized by John is as solid a piece of history as his crucifixion under Pontius Pilate. A church which existed in some degree of rivalry with a John the Baptist sect would never have invented a tradition of Jesus' receiving at John's hands a baptism which was everywhere understood as a sign of repentance for sin. That the baptism was a turning point for Jesus which brought to an end his years of obscurity in Nazareth and prepared him in a decisive way for his ministry is evident from the fact that what happened then had the same relation to his ministry as Paul's experience on the Damascus road had to his Gentile mission, or Jeremiah's call to the years of his prophetic task.

The Fourth Gospel suggests that this one encounter was of some duration, a period which Jesus spent in the company of John, and on this basis some scholars have let their imaginations run freely and have reconstructed not only a time in which Jesus was a disciple of John but also a rupture of their relationship when Jesus finally decided to follow a different course. It is safer to hold by the little that we know: that Jesus recognized John as a prophet sent by God to recall a wayward Israel to its destiny as the people of God; that as a true son of Israel he went down to the Jordan to validate in baptism his solidarity with John's new Israel of God; that Jesus in spite of all that he had in common with John could not make common cause with him but had to make a fresh beginning; and that John, whatever hopes he had for Jesus, had sufficient questions in his mind concerning him that, although some of his disciples transferred their allegiance to Jesus, he had no intention of merging his mission with that of Jesus. The relation between the two has in it very clearly both a measure of mutual recognition and a measure of tension and disagreement.

THEIR MUTUAL RECOGNITION OF EACH OTHER

The radical subordination of John to Jesus in many passages in the Gospels conceals the fact that to many in the Palestine of that day John must have been by far the more impressive figure. His dramatic appearance in the garb of an Elijah, with a coat of camel's hair and a leather loincloth; his ascetic diet of desert fare of locusts and wild honey and his frequent fasts; his warning of the nearness of a fiery judgment day that struck terror into men's hearts; his insult to Jewish pride in demanding of every Israelite a baptism like proselyte baptism in which the whole of one's past life should be washed away; above all, his success in drawing great crowds out of the towns and villages of Palestine; and finally, his prophetic courage in rebuking a king for his immorality—all made him a most striking and unforgettable phenomenon. No such prophet had been seen in the nation for more than five hundred years. No one would ever have thought of classifying John with the rabbis. In comparison, Jesus' ministry must have seemed very tame. There was nothing in his dress to mark him as different from any other man (a point concealed in pictures by the predilection of artists to give him distinctive clothing), and he ate and drank what other men ate and drank. In fact, he made no secret of his enjoyment of good food and wine and his dislike of fasting. He put far more emphasis upon the joy and blessing of life in the Kingdom of God that was ready at any moment to break in upon men than upon the terrors of hellfire on the Judgment Day. His manner of teaching made many people think of him more as a new kind of rabbi than as a successor of the prophets. And so far as converts were concerned he was a dismal failure in comparison with John. There may have been crowds to hear him at times in Galilee, but when he finished his mission there he had only a handful of followers. It is little wonder then that in some minds Jesus was subordinated to John and the demand was made upon him that he conform his conduct and his practices to those of John (Matt. 9:14 ff.). To the popular mind John undoubtedly seemed to be the more serious-minded and the stricter man of God. Jesus had to defend his freedom to be himself and to have his own mission in distinction from John, but he did not let himself be set in rivalry to John.

Against this background we can understand how inevitable it would be that Jesus should be forced from time to time to clarify his relation with John and that John should have had a questioning attitude concerning Jesus, as appears in Luke 7:18 ff. That John should have had any doubts whether Jesus was the Messiah seems to contradict the unanimous tradition of the early church that John's chief function was to point forward to the advent of Jesus as the Messiah. Luke's birth story has the unborn John in his mother's womb recognizing as his Lord the unborn Jesus in Mary's womb! Matthew has John at the baptism of Jesus recognize him as Messiah and protest that Jesus should in the true order of things baptize him, John. The Fourth Gospel has John testify that he saw the Spirit descending upon Jesus in the form of a dove, thereby marking him as the Messiah. But if John from

the time of the baptism knew Jesus as the Messiah with such
certainty, why did he not become his first disciple and merge his
movement with that of Jesus, and how could he be thrown into
uncertainty at any later time? We can understand these traditions only as later developments as the church pondered the relation of John to Jesus, but there may well have been a basis for
them in that one encounter of John with Jesus, a recognition by
John that he was confronted with a man of God who towered far
beyond himself. Jesus had a profound respect for the prophetic
stature of John: "not a mother's son greater than John" (Matt.
11:11). Would John with his prophet's sensitivity be unaware of
how far beyond him in the things of God ranged the mind and
spirit of Jesus? Is it even conceivable that he would not ask
himself the question: Is this perhaps the Messiah? But the
Messiah for him was One who would bring speedily the Day of
Judgment and final redemption, not one who would only preach,
teach, heal, and drive out demons. It is significant that when
John sent from prison to ask whether Jesus was the Messiah,
Jesus' answer consisted of quotations from Servant passages in
Isaiah which foreshadowed the very nature of his mission (Matt.
11:2–6). Neither John nor any of his Jewish contemporaries
identified the Messiah with the Servant of Second Isaiah or at-
tributed anything of the character of the Servant to the Messiah.
Their Messiah was a conquering king, not a Suffering Servant.

THEIR CONTEXT IN THE PROPHETIC TRADITION

In order to get John and Jesus in proper perspective we need
to draw out a time line and place on it the whole succession of
prophetic figures in Israel. The line begins with Moses in the
thirteenth century B.C., and for five hundred years we catch only
glimpses from time to time of the prophets who sustained it
through those centuries. Only those who spoke at some critical
moment in the history have been remembered in the tradition.
Then for two and a half centuries, from the middle of the eighth
to the end of the sixth, a series of great prophets stand forth in
full view as a consequence of their disciples preserving a written

record of their preaching. Strangely, as Israel became a church scattered across the whole of the Near East and began to cherish as never before the records of its faith from the past, prophetic voices faltered and then fell silent, with serious consequences for Judaism. A better understanding of the prophetic writings would have taught them that the word of God to which the prophets witnessed calls constantly for fresh and living witness in new situations. The word from the past has ever to become the living word in the present moment. For more than five hundred years there was no prophet in Israel and men came to think that in their Scriptures they now possessed the whole of God's counsel so that there was no need of any further prophet. Into that later situation came John the Baptist, a prophet whose stature placed him directly in line with the greatest prophets of the past. (Perhaps one day the community that he established near the Jordan will be discovered, as Qumran was, and we may even have a book of his sermons, confronting us with the dilemma of whether to introduce it into the Old Testament or into the New!) But successful as he was with the common people and great as was his stature as a prophet of Israel, John was never taken up into the traditions of Judaism, and the remembrance of him has been preserved mainly in Christian literature.

Then came Jesus, closely upon the heels of John, in many of his characteristics in direct continuity with the Old Testament prophets, and in particular with the last great one, Second Isaiah: his mission a restoration of Israel to its destiny as the servant people of God, his gospel a heralding of the new day that must dawn for a people that will let its sins be forgiven, his preaching a planting in men of that word of God which in Second Isaiah had in it power to renew the whole earth (Isa. 55:10–13), his parables a perfecting of the prophetic parable that exposed men to God's judgment in spite of themselves. John was Elijah reborn, but in Jesus it was as though the whole succession of the prophets had been gathered up, embodied in him, and carried forward to an undreamed-of climax. They spoke the word and lived for it no matter what it cost. So too did Jesus, but in a mysterious way he *was* the word he spoke. Word and life were one in him. He was the goal to which the whole prophetic succession had been pointed from the beginning. Unfortunately this perspective in which John and Jesus belong is destroyed when Old and New Testament are split apart and the two climactic figures in the prophetic succession are separated from the body of the movement. One has only to think of the many volumes on the subject "The Prophets of Israel," from which both John and Jesus are excluded, or the interpretations of Jesus which so overemphasize his context in the Judaism of his day or the uniqueness of the gospel which came to birth through him, that the Old Testament loses its continuity with the New!

John the Baptist is the linchpin between the two Testaments. He is a prophet of Israel with a valid right to a place in the Old Testament. We have no alternative but to say that his exclusion from Judaism and the failure of Judaism to give him a place in its sacred scriptures was as serious a denial of divine revelation as would have been a similar exclusion of Jeremiah or Isaiah. And yet John and Jesus stand shoulder to shoulder in the service of the same Word of God. Jesus affirmed his unity with John more than once. Being baptized by him was a most impressive indication of solidarity with him. On another occasion, when the two were criticized, John as a fanatic because of his asceticism, and Jesus as a glutton because of his enjoyment of his meals, Jesus chided the critics for their childish arbitrariness and in the phrase, "God's wisdom is justified in all her children" (Matt. 11:19), took his place alongside John as a child of the same wisdom, or word, of God which had brought John to birth. In this assertion he spoke out in behalf of the freedom of every son or servant of the Word to discharge his task in his own distinctive way. The differences between John and Jesus did not in any way negate their unity in the ongoing work of God. Again, when Jesus' authority was challenged by some of the religious leaders (Luke 20:1 ff.), he tested their ability to discern the kind of authority which he exercised by questioning them concerning their attitude toward John. "Did John have God's authority for his demand that every Jew should submit to his baptism of repentance?" The respect of the masses for John is

evident in the reaction of the leaders. They were unwilling to
grant John the authority of a true prophet of God, for they still
rejected his demand upon them, and yet they would not admit
openly their repudiation of him for fear of offending the people.
With such men it was hopeless and useless for Jesus to enter
upon any discussion of his authority. But his answer points once
more to the profound unity between himself and John of which
he was conscious and of which he made no secret.

Jesus was well aware that what was happening both in John's
mission and in his own was a rebirth of the prophetic line and a
taking-up anew of the prophetic task. We must not think of the
line as ending with Jesus. It is noteworthy that when he speaks
of himself as servant, undoubtedly with the servant of Isa., chs.
40 to 66, in mind in whom was incorporated the whole agelong
prophetic destiny and function of Israel as Servant of the Word,
he always reaches out and takes his disciples in with him into
the servant task. So also Paul in Phil., ch. 2, when he portrays
Jesus as servant, does so in order to incite the church to find its
destiny in the servant image. Jesus in his person and in his
mission brought the prophetic function to its climactic fulfillment and at the same time transformed it, committing it to his
disciples in its transformed character, so that the ministry of the
church is in continuity with his ministry only when there lives
ever afresh in it this transformed prophetic character.

A COMPARISON

We must not let the sharp differences between John and
Jesus blind us to the elements they had in common. The Gospel
of Matthew uses identical words to summarize both the preaching of John and the earliest preaching of Jesus, "Repent, for the
Kingdom of Heaven is at hand" (Matt. 3:2; 4:17). As we shall
see, there was a difference between John's and Jesus' proclamation of the Kingdom's nearness, but it must have required more
than ordinary discernment in the hearers to detect the difference.
What would be most obvious would be how different both were
from the rabbis. They too had something to say about the com-

ing of the Kingdom and their whole religion was based on the conviction that by obedience to the law of God they could make the Kingdom come. If for one day, they said, all Israel would keep the law, the great new age would dawn. But this was a reversal of prophetic teaching. The law in the Old Testament defined the obedience of a community that within the covenant relation was responding with wholehearted love to the love of God. Faithfulness to God came first and the expression of that faithfulness was obedience to God's will in the concrete situations of community life. The prophets knew that until the heart was right with God a man was incapable of an honest obedience and was prone to justify himself by obeying a selection of laws, which left him undisturbed in his most serious disobedience to God. Therefore the prophets' call was before all else for a repentance, a turning about of the whole man, a return of man to the God from whom his sins had alienated him. The personal covenant relation with God had to be restored before there could be a fulfillment of the law. Only thus could Israel be truly Israel and ready for the coming of the Kingdom. John's aim was to bring every Israelite to a repentance that would restore him to his place in the true Israel. But sometimes we forget that Jesus, too, saw his mission in his lifetime as limited to the "lost sheep of the house of Israel," a restoration of Israel to its true nature and destiny as the people of God, which would then mean that it would be the light of the world (Isa. 49:6; Matt. 5:14).

Both John and Jesus saw only a short time remaining for Israel to repent. The last days were at hand. God's patience with an evil generation was near exhaustion. Soon he would intervene in judgment and in mercy to bring both faithfulness and unfaithfulness to their appropriate reward. John may have emphasized the terror of that day and Jesus the blessing of it, but it had both sides for both of them. It is sheer sentimentalism to ignore the prophetic note of judgment in Jesus' preaching. His prediction of the destruction of the Temple, echoed by Stephen, is directly parallel with Jeremiah's similar prediction and, like it, must be understood as a rejection of a religious order that was blinding the people to their true state before God.

Both John and Jesus, with their diagnosis of the nation's sickness as apostasy from God, included religious and irreligious alike in their indictment and refused to recognize the well-established line of demarcation between righteous and sinners, thereby infuriating those who were confident of their righteousness and earning a warm response from a wide range of persons who stood on the outside of religion. They were neither of them friends of the "establishment" and it is not surprising that they were so warmly received by those who had long felt the deprivation of being excluded from the religious community.

The dramatic rite of baptism as a sign of putting off the old life and putting on the new was practiced in both missions, but with a difference which, we shall see, points directly at the uniqueness of Jesus' gospel. There is good reason to trust the note in the Fourth Gospel that although Jesus' disciples baptized, Jesus did not (John 4:2), for we find the same restraint in Paul who performed the ceremony of baptism himself only in exceptional circumstances (I Cor. 1:13–17). Paul attributes his restraint to the specific commission of Christ to him to preach the gospel. The ancient world was full of religious ceremonies which were expected to effect a spiritual change in those who submitted to them, in some instances even to transform them from men into gods. We know from historical records how soon Christians began to regard baptism as of itself performing the work of divine grace, cleansing the initiate of his sin and assuring him of God's favor. It was most likely to guard against the development of this false sacramentalism that neither Jesus nor Paul made it their practice to perform the ceremony themselves but placed all their emphasis upon the preaching of the word in which God brings men to a true repentance and cleansing.

Both John and Jesus had disciples who were trained to extend and carry forward the mission of their master. We get a glimpse of John's converse with his disciples in the report that he trained them to pray, which impelled Jesus' disciples to ask him to do the same for them. This suggests also some measure of communication between the two groups, which was only to be expected, since some disciples of Jesus had begun as disciples of

John. Their transfer from the one group to the other may have taken place when John was imprisoned. Or again, they may have been with John only for a time and were back at their normal occupations when Jesus found them and recognized their usefulness for his mission. The Synoptics and the Fourth Gospel preserve, perhaps with good reason, variant traditions of how these disciples of John became disciples of Jesus. But the step from the one group to the other was, in spite of all elements that the two had in common, a step from the Old Testament to the New.

We turn now to the distinction between John and Jesus, which should help us to see more clearly the distinction between the Old Testament and the New. Just as Jeremiah reached forward toward a day when there would be a new covenant relation between God and man and God would write his law in men's hearts, so also John was conscious of a work of God that lay beyond all that he as a prophet could do. He could call men to repentance and baptize them with a baptism of repentance, but this only prepared the way for a profounder baptism, with the Holy Spirit and with fire. The significance of fire in this connection is uncertain. It could be the fire of judgment, but more likely here, as in many passages in the Old Testament, fire represents the presence of the living God, making doubly clear that baptism with the Spirit means nothing less than baptism with God. John prepared men for God's coming, but in the Last Day, God himself would come and men would be immersed not just in water but in the presence and power of God.

BAPTISM WITH THE SPIRIT

Every facet of the New Testament witness points back to an event, either in Jesus' person or through him in a community of persons, which constituted a new beginning for humanity. Paul's "new man in Christ" is paralleled by the Fourth Gospel's "man born of the Spirit" and Luke's new age of the Spirit. The conviction of all three and of the churches which they represent was that the baptism with the Spirit for which John hoped had begun with Jesus' ministry. It is widely assumed in New Testament scholarship today, however, that for Jesus as for John the new age was wholly future, that Jesus announced its imminence and prepared men for its coming but that his relation to its coming was almost identical with that of John. All representations in the Gospels of the age of the Spirit as beginning with Jesus, and of his being conscious of its beginning with him as in the account of his baptism, are then interpreted as a reading back of the later development into Jesus' ministry. Jesus is regarded as having had no consciousness of the magnitude of the event of which he was the center! How, then, did Christian baptism come to be so sharply distinguished from John's baptism at such an early date? For Paul, baptism is a dying and rising again with Christ from which the Christian comes forth endowed with the same Spirit of God that was the empowering Spirit of Jesus' ministry. We have to ask ourselves whether baptism as performed by the disciples in Jesus' lifetime was merely a continuation of John's baptism unmarked by any distinction between Jesus and John. It is strange that in the Synoptic Gospels there is no mention of Jesus or the disciples baptizing and that in Jesus' instructions to the Twelve and to the Seventy when he sent them out there was no command to baptize. Yet water baptism is so firmly rooted in the Christian movement from the beginning that it seems inconceivable that it should have begun only after Jesus' death and resurrection.

The clue to the mystery seems to be in Paul's attitude toward baptism in which he accepts it as the established initiatory rite for Christians and yet in general makes a point of refraining from baptizing anyone. He says that he is following the explicit command of Jesus, and we may assume also the example of Jesus, in making the preaching of the gospel his one concern. Baptism with the Spirit, for Paul as for the Fourth Gospel, came through the hearing of the Word. God's Word could never be rightly heard and received as the word of life unless in it God himself came to man and took possession of his very being. The Spirit was that form of God's presence in which he was able to indwell man's self. But are Spirit and Word inseparable for Paul and for the Fourth Gospel but not for Jesus? Even Second Isaiah knows that the word of God that falls like rain upon the deserts of human life has in it the life-transforming power of God himself. The word that Jesus sows in men's lives has hidden in it God's new age. To receive the word is to be already in a new relation with God that one day will flower into the full life of the Kingdom. The fact that where water baptism was central for John the preaching of the gospel is central for Jesus and water baptism falls into the background certainly suggests that baptism into God, i.e., with the Spirit of God, was already with Jesus, and not just with his successors, that which distinguished his mission from that of John.

In this light the representation of Jesus' baptism as different from all other preceding baptisms in that he was baptized not only with water but with the Spirit, and the fact that in the Fourth Gospel, The Acts, and the letters of Paul, Christian baptism differs from John's baptism in that it is baptism with water *and* the Spirit (John 3:5; Acts 19:1–7; I Cor. 12:13), take on unusual significance. So also does the constant emphasis that Jesus' preaching, healing, and exorcising of demons is in the power of the Spirit, and the insistence of the author of Acts that the achievements of the early church were due not to the talents or wisdom or earnestness of the first Christians but to the presence and power of God's Spirit working in them in spite of their deficiencies. The claim of every part of the New Testament is that the presence of God with man for which John hoped was actuality in Jesus, and through him in those who by faith were bonded together with him. They shared with him his new relation of Sonship with God and were indwelt and empowered by the same Spirit of God that was the secret of his unique life. Far from being merely another preparer of the way for the new age of the Spirit, Jesus was in himself the incarnation of the new age, the miracle of a human life in which the gulf between God and man was bridged, the reality on earth of God with man and man with God, a self fulfilled and freed to live by having as its center the living God himself, a man so one with God that the love and truth and holiness of God were imaged in every segment of his existence. One needs to guard the phrase "indwelt by the Spirit" against mystical and superstitious misinterpretation, recognizing that it expresses not a localizing of God within the human body but rather the intimacy of a personal relationship. It is like Paul's use of the terms "in Christ" and "Christ in me" to describe his relation with Jesus Christ. Even for Jesus there is no merging of the human and the divine. His relation with the Father is personal and is sustained in prayer and obedience. Yet this distinction between human and divine is no obstacle to the most perfect oneness between Father and Son, and the word "Spirit" seems to be the name for this oneness in which the Sovereign God becomes the living center of a human self, the perfect obedience of that self being the outward manifestation of the hidden sovereignty.

It seems absurd to think that Jesus was unconscious of the magnitude of the new age that had its origin with him or of the distance that separated him from John. His whole mission was at stake when, against those who thought his movement would be more impressive if it were more like John's, he defended his right to pour his new wine into new bottles. For John the Kingdom was wholly future, near but not yet present, but for Jesus the Kingdom was both present and future. Those who make Jesus' eschatology purely futurist, like John's, ignore the remarkable parallels between Jesus' preaching and the preaching of Second Isaiah and the possibility of Jesus' eschatology having more in common with that of the prophet than with the contemporary Jewish apocalypticism. Second Isaiah, like Jesus, has an intense expectation that at any moment the day may dawn when God's sovereignty will be established openly over the whole earth and his age-long purpose vindicated. But already in the present, where to the outward eye evil men seem to be more powerful than the faithful and God seems absent, those whose ears are open to God's word have had his sovereignty over man's life revealed to them and are able to live with confidence and joy in the light of that as yet hidden sovereignty. The Kingdom, hidden in the present moment, will shortly be revealed to the eyes of all mankind, a day of terror for some and of blessing for others. In line with this prophetic eschatology, Jesus' Kingdom is present hiddenly in the world wherever men are open to the word in which God comes to them. There is an imminent day of judgment and redemption when the Kingdom will no longer be hidden, but men do not have to wait for the Kingdom to come at some future day. The day of God's coming is *now* in his gospel. God is not distant. God is present. God's dwelling place is not in a remote heaven but with man. And man's only true existence, the existence in which he is whole, is himself, is truly human, is one of unconditional openness to the presence of God with him. The source of all his misery, brokenness, and sin is his absence from the God who is never absent from him but only hidden by his human blindness and willfulness. He cannot be himself until in the place of rule within him, self abdicates and God becomes sovereign. But the establishment of that sovereignty and the coming of the Kingdom are just two ways of describing the same reality, and a third way is to say that the man is indwelt by the Spirit of God, baptized with the Spirit, or born of the Spirit.

Another pointer in the same direction is the way in which Jesus speaks of faith. It has frequently been noted that he omits any mention of the object of faith and attributes to the faith itself transforming power. "If you have faith as a grain of mustard seed, you will say to this mountain, Be removed." "Your faith has saved you; go in peace." This has sometimes been interpreted as though man's faith had in it of itself a power to save. It does surprise us that Jesus should say, "Your faith has saved you" rather than "The grace and mercy of God has saved you." But faith for Jesus was an openness to God in which the barriers were down between God and man and God was with man in such a way that his forgiving love and renewing power were the core of the man's existence. To have faith was to be restored to the relation with God for which man was created, to be the "Thou" to God's "I," to be the earthly imaging of the very nature of God himself, or, to use another New Testament phrase which says the same thing, to be on earth a responsive and responsible son of the Father in heaven. Thus, Jesus expected of his disciples that they would "be like God," forgiving those who offended them with the same unlimited forgiveness which they themselves had found in God, caring for men in their need not according to their deserving but with compassion for all just as God sends his rain on the just and the unjust. The Sermon on the Mount as a description of the Christian life is incomprehensible unless we understand that Jesus is describing the life of men who have entered the age of the Spirit and are centered no longer in self but in the Spirit of God.

The fruit of coming under God's immediate sovereignty in this way was a joyful recognition of the world as God's world and all things in it as God's provision for man's life. Letting God be sovereign in his own creation brought with it a freedom from anxiety about things but also a freedom from any suspicion that evil resided in things of themselves. To live in the world as God's Kingdom was to be at home in the world (to "inherit the earth") and to enjoy it. Therefore, Jesus' refusal to follow John in his asceticism was not just a minor difference in "style of life" but was an essential expression of man's new life in God and in God's world.

It would appear, then, that when the early church represented John as the forerunner of Jesus, the preparer of the way, it was doing no violence to John but rather was discerning his true relation to Jesus better than John himself had ever understood it in his lifetime. John was the herald of the new age when the Messiah would set God's Spirit in men's hearts. John may have been unable to recognize the age of the Spirit in its hidden beginnings, his conception of it differing from the actuality, but it stretches credibility entirely too far to suppose that Jesus, too, was unable to recognize it when it was the reality of his own existence and the gift that above all else he was concerned in his mission to bestow upon men. On the last night of his life he concentrated his entire purpose into the simple act of breaking bread and giving it to his disciples as a symbol of the life in God that was his own and that he existed to give to them. Bread in Isa., ch. 55, is the word of God which has in it God's power to transform man's life. "This is my body" in Hebrew terms means "This is myself," and Jesus' self was his life in the Word and in the Spirit. It took his death and resurrection to make men open to what he came to give them, but, unless we deny to him the words "This is my body," we must surely grant to him the knowledge that what was being fulfilled in him and in his ministry was the new age of the Spirit anticipated and predicted by John. It was, therefore, no belittling of John when Jesus, having said of John "none greater born of woman," went on to say that "he who is least in the Kingdom of God is greater than John" (Luke 7:28). He was not comparing John with Peter or Levi but was emphasizing sharply the wholly new dimension of life in the new age that was dawning.

Chapter II

JESUS, THE PHARISEE,
AND THE WOMAN WHO WAS A SINNER

IT IS PECULIAR THAT COMMENTATORS on Luke 7:36–50 generally have insisted that the woman in this story was a prostitute.
The translators of *The New English Bible* are so sure of it that
they render the phrase, "a woman who was living an immoral
life in the town." The supposition has furnished countless
preachers with a springboard from which to reconstruct a
dramatic picture of the woman's degradation. But the Greek
words used in the story to describe the woman do not necessarily have that meaning at all. They say simply that in the
sharply divided religious order of the community she was classified as a sinner in distinction from such righteous persons as
Simon. The story tells us nothing about the nature of her sin.
Jesus' parable, in representing her sin as ten times as great as
Simon's, reflects merely the magnitude of her offenses against
the law in comparison with the scrupulous correctness of Simon's
life. Jesus grants to Simon the greatness of the distance between
himself and the woman so far as the keeping of the law is concerned but only that he may then turn on him and fasten upon
him the fact that he and the woman are both sinners, both bankrupts before God, both helpless to save themselves without God's
forgiveness. It is not Jesus but Simon who emphasizes the
woman's sinfulness. To Jesus both are equally sinners. Why,
then, has interpretation not been content to leave the matter
there but has instead exerted itself to magnify the woman's sin?
One unfortunate result (or perhaps this is unconsciously the

desired result) is that it prevents decent respectable people in the Christian congregation from identifying themselves with the woman in her encounter with Jesus.

SINNERS AND PHARISEES

If we would do justice to the terms "righteous" and "sinner" in their New Testament usage, we must first know something of the religious and social order in the first-century Jewish community. Both "Pharisee" and "sinner" are widely misinterpreted. For many Christians, "Pharisee" is in common usage a synonym for "hypocrite." The word conjures up a picture of a very disagreeable type of religious person, shallow, boastful, spiritually dishonest, insufferably complacent and pretentious. The antagonism between the early church and Pharisaic Judaism has tended to accentuate the polemic against the Pharisees in the New Testament tradition, so that it is possible to draw a quite false impression from it. But the New Testament picture is not by any means unanimously of this character. Nicodemus is no hypocrite. He is a deeply earnest believer in God, well versed in the Scriptures and eager to learn from Jesus whatever he can. Gamaliel in Acts 5:34 ff. is an eminently fair-minded man who refuses to be carried away by the popular sentiment against the Christians. Paul in his pre-Christian days was a splendid representative of Pharisaism: imbued with a single-minded devotion to God and to Israel as the people of God; a student of Scripture and tradition as the revelation of God's law for man which must be unconditionally obeyed; scrupulous in the keeping of the law, so that he considered himself blameless; the enemy of all who ignored or broke any part of the law, since in doing so they were endangering the very existence of Israel; a regular participant in the worship of the synagogue. Pharisees were noted for their generosity to the poor. They also, as Jesus recognized in his portrait of them in Luke 18:9 ff., went beyond the requirements of the law in such spiritual disciplines as fasting. They were models of religious devotion and moral seriousness.

Some scholars, such as Travers Herford,[3] in their attempt to give a fair historical description of the Pharisees, find it impossible to believe that Jesus should ever have spoken harshly of them as he is represented doing in the Gospels. They interpret these seemingly unfair polemics as coming from the later period in the church when Judaism and Christianity were rivals for the allegiance of men in the Roman Empire, polemics that have unfortunately been attributed to Jesus. But behind this interpretation there is an assumption that Jesus could not possibly have been so critical of men who were earnestly religious and moral. The apologists for the Pharisees might have considered the antithesis between Paul the Pharisee and Paul the Christian. Paul was fully aware of all the values of Pharisaic religion. For a time it had seemed to him that the Christian movement was endangering everything that made life worth living in its questioning of the established order in Judaism. But when the life of the new age of the Spirit became God's gift to him in Jesus Christ, he saw the whole legalistic system of Pharisaism as a means by which men justified themselves before God and in their self-righteousness became impervious to both judgment and grace. Paul opposed Judaistic Christianity for years because he saw in it a revised form, a semi-Christianized form, of the self-justifying religion which he himself had known in his earlier days. Paul and Jesus stand together in their antithesis to Pharisaism, not because all Pharisees were hypocrites, but simply because the life in God which is man's only true life has to be God's gracious gift to him in the midst of his unworthiness and sinfulness, and the one insuperable barrier to its realization is man's confidence that by his religious devotion and moral earnestness he has already established for himself adequate credit with God. Any suggestion that Jesus' teaching was only a slightly revised form of contemporary Pharisaic teaching, the attitude of Harvie Branscomb in *Jesus and the Law of Moses,*[4] fails to grasp the central point of his mission. He came to establish a new relation, a new covenant, between God and man, to bring God out of a distant heaven and a distant future and to set him in men's hearts as the Sovereign of their entire existence, under whose immediate sovereignty they would find their freedom to be truly men. The greatest hindrance to his mission he found not in the sins of the sinners but in the already established righteousness of the righteous. They were so zealous in their keeping of the law that they were no longer conscious of their own sin or of their need for forgiveness. They were so confident of their own righteousness that they were continually sitting in judgment on other men. They were so anxious to preserve their own purity that they withheld themselves from contact with Gentiles and with all those Jews who for any reason were careless about the keeping of the law.

Against this background we begin to see how the word "sinner" was defined in New Testament times. The "righteous" were those who, like Paul the Pharisee, held themselves to a strict observance of the hundreds of laws and regulations which were to be found in Scripture and tradition. The "sinners" were those who for any reason refused to conform to that religious program. They were not necessarily bad people. The most virtuous Gentile was officially a sinner because he did not live in accord with the Jewish law. Socrates in the categories of the Pharisees would be classified as a sinner! Anyone who rebelled against the burdensomeness of a legalistic religion and went his own way was branded a sinner. There were Greek cities scattered all through Palestine on both sides of the Jordan, with Greek theaters, gymnasiums, and schools of philosophy, and any Jew who let himself be led away by Greek culture into a Hellenized life was a sinner. Men who gathered taxes for the Roman Government were regarded as traitors to their own nation and therefore sinners. It can be seen thus that the word comprehended a wide spectrum of people and that it did not by any means signify an immoral or irresponsible life. The one thing that all "sinners" had in common was their exclusion from the synagogue and from the Jewish religious community. The Pharisees drew a sharp dividing line between the righteous and the sinners and, of course, assumed that God belonged with the righteous on their side of the dividing line. Jesus offended them deeply when he refused to recognize the validity of the line, treated men on both sides of it as sinners in need of God's forgiveness and increasingly spent his time in the company of what, if we would avoid misunderstanding, we should call "outsiders" rather than "sinners."

THE ENCOUNTER

To a modern reader the story in Luke 7:36 ff. is incredible. When guests come to dinner, the door is closed and locked and only they and their hosts are found in the room. Gate-crashers might gain entrance to a cocktail party but not to a dinner. But in the ancient East customs were very different. William Manson[5] notes that in the "Arabian Nights" uninvited persons enter a house when they hear the sound of music coming from it. Poor people might find their way into a place where a dinner was being served and wait in the shadows at the side of the room in hope that some leftovers from the feast might be thrown to them. As the setting of our story we must picture a series of couches for the guests, all pointed inward toward a central table, with the guests reclining, their feet in the shadows and their heads in the light. Thus, the woman kneeling at Jesus' feet would not be particularly conspicuous until Simon's interest drew attention to her.

Simon's invitation to Jesus must be attributed wholly to curiosity and not to any measure of respect or genuine interest. He wanted to see this phenomenon from Nazareth at closer range. The discourtesy of omitting the kiss of greeting, the water to wash his dusty feet, and the oil for his head was meant to show that Jesus was not being received as a friend or as an equal. It is interesting that Jesus accepted the invitation in spite of his awareness of how uncongenial the Pharisaic mind could be to him—an indication that even where he was accustomed to find a wall of resistance and hostility he was willing to ply his mission and to risk insult in order to forward his purpose.

G. B. Caird[6] and Joachim Jeremias[7] both assume a prior contact between Jesus and the woman. Caird is cautious: "She had seen and heard him from the fringe of the crowd." Jeremias is

bolder and imagines that Simon and his friends as well as the
woman had that very day heard Jesus preach a sermon on forgiveness. These are surmises which argue validly that the devotion of the woman to Jesus must have been her response to
what he had already meant to her. What form that contact took
we cannot know. It is sufficient that the woman was aware he
was the friend of people such as herself and gave fresh hope to
men and women who were in despair about their lives. Whether
she gained this knowledge directly or from someone who had
been helped by him, we have to leave uncertain, but certainly
she did not perform her act of devotion in ignorance of who he
was or of what she might expect from him. It is likely that her
unconventional act was in part inspired by observing the discourtesies of Simon to Jesus when he arrived at the house.

There have been arguments about the unity of the passage.
S. M. Gilmour, in his exegesis in *The Interpreter's Bible*,[8] claims
that two distinct traditions have been woven together to form the
present story, the parable having one point and the remainder
of the story another. But this rests upon a misreading of the
story. Gilmour asserts as the theme of the story: "Love is the
qualification for divine forgiveness. . . . One who loves much is
forgiven much," and then finds in the parable the exact reverse,
that one who is forgiven much will love much. This attributes to
the story an unusual concept of forgiveness, to be found nowhere
else in the New Testament, that men are forgiven by God according to the degree in which they show love. But it also fails
to see that, when Jesus points out the abundance of the woman's
love and the absence of Simon's, he is driving home the point of
his parable, that the response to forgiveness is love. He is not
introducing a new theme, that love merits forgiveness. The opening words of v. 47, translated "wherefore" in KJV, and the
phrase "for she loved much" have been responsible for this false
impression, though the concluding phrase "to whom little is forgiven, the same loveth little" should have been sufficient to indi-
cate that here as in the parable the love is the fruit and proof of
the reception of forgiveness. The NEB has guarded against mis-

understanding by translating the verse: "And so, I tell you, her great love proves that her many sins have been forgiven; where little has been forgiven, little love is shown." Jesus' declaration in v. 48, "Your sins are forgiven" is thus a validation publicly of a forgiveness which is already reality and has shown its fruits before them all, not a granting of forgiveness on the basis of the love that has been shown.

Bultmann in his *History of the Synoptic Tradition*[9] discounts the possibility of the story's being a remembrance of an actual encounter, regarding it as a construction that grew up round the parable and its application in v. 47, "Everything else has been constructed as realistic background on the basis of Mark 14:3–9, a passage Luke there omits." A comparison of Mark 14:3–9 with the present story shows only slight resemblances but sufficient to explain why Luke might omit the former when he was including the latter. But it is not at all convincing evidence that Luke constructed a setting for his parable out of Mark 14:3–9. Must one be so skeptical about anything definite being remembered concerning Jesus' encounters with different types of people? The whole story has about it a vividness that makes one receptive to Plummer's assertion in the International Critical Commentary[10]: "The conduct both of Jesus and of the woman is unlike either fiction or clumsily distorted fact. His gentle severity towards Simon and tender reception of the sinner are as much beyond the reach of invention as the eloquence of her speechless affection." The whole story, when rightly understood, is so much of a piece and forms such a perfect setting for the parable that it should require more convincing evidence than has been produced to negate the possibility that Jesus has been remembered in a two-sided encounter. Undoubtedly, the story has had its edges rounded in transmission. The last two verses occur in other settings and may have been transferred from there to here. But the body of the account has a rocklike solidity in which each part fits so perfectly into the whole and the response of Jesus to the Pharisee on the one hand and to the woman on the other are in such agreement with what we know of him from other sources that we may have reasonable confidence that what appears before us is a genuine historical encounter. This is what he was like.

The use of the prophetic parable in order to get past a man's defenses is typical of Jesus. We shall see it again and look at it more carefully in the story of his encounter with the lawyer to whom he spoke the parable of the good Samaritan. The parables are so often regarded as illustrations of religious truth, or little stories to make Jesus' meaning concrete for people who could not grasp the truth in any other form, that the cunning and the cutting force of the prophetic parable remains unrecognized. The classic form of it appears in II Sam., ch. 12, where Nathan uses it to bring King David to his senses. The prophet tells a story which has its victim hidden in it. The story presents to the listener an objective case and calls for his judgment upon the person or persons in it. The listener pronounces his honest judgment and then discovers, when it is too late, that hidden under the figures in the story is his own situation. He had been tricked into pronouncing God's judgment upon himself. It is peculiar that none of the commentaries on our passage note Jesus' use of this type of prophetic parable here. Yet its recognition is essential if we are to get the full flavor of the incident. Jesus, confronted with a man who is so confident of his own righteousness that he judges other persons harshly and is impervious to any suggestion that he himself might need forgiveness, draws out of his armory his sharpest weapon with which to cut through the callous blindness of the man. The parable, which must have been designed on the spur of the moment, speaks to the situation perfectly and at the same time has in it a depth of meaning which makes it continue to speak through all the ages. We marvel at the mind that could produce such a parable at a moment's notice. At the same time we find in it a mark of how Jesus took up into himself the heritage of the prophets.

We are not told anything of the conversation between Jesus and his fellow guests as they reclined at the table in Simon's house. The spotlight is focused on Simon, Jesus, and the woman. The woman was not present by accident. She had come because she had learned that Jesus was to be there. The oil of myrrh which she had brought with her and which was to be expended in anointing Jesus' feet was an indication that already before the act in Simon's house she had her reasons for gratitude toward him. Her tears show how deeply she had been moved by what he had done for her. It was regarded as disgraceful for a woman to unloose her hair in the presence of men but she was so carried away by her devotion that she did not care what anyone might think of her.

Simon was shocked that Jesus permitted the woman's extravagant act of devotion. He said nothing, but his reaction was so evident in his face that no words were necessary to express it. What was happening to the woman, why she was so moved, was of no interest to him. He could see only a person who plainly belonged among the untouchable sinners being allowed to embrace the feet of one of his guests. Simon had been curious to know if perhaps Jesus might be a prophet, but Jesus' permission of this defiling act was proof that he had not the spiritual discernment even of a good Pharisee, much less of a prophet. The possibility that Jesus should have a mission to such people as this to restore them to their true life in God and that what was there before the eyes of all was an instance of his accomplishment of his mission was completely beyond the comprehension of Simon. There was no place in his theology for a ministry of reconciliation that would bring healing to a broken and despairing humanity.

Jesus had been aware of Simon's displeasure for some time before he spoke. The discourtesies on his arrival had warned him what to expect. The woman's act had let him know that he had one impassioned ally in the room. He was aware how vulnerable her act had made her in such a company and at the same time he knew that for her this was the public confession of her new-found faith. We can imagine the joy that he felt that his gospel of forgiveness had found its proper goal in her and had brought a life-changing faith to birth. God was at work here overthrowing the power of evil, establishing his Kingdom on earth in the midst of human need, and these men who claimed to be the spiritual leaders of Israel had no eyes to see it. All about him Jesus had men who in the complacency of their religiosity and self-righteousness were utterly blind to God and to all that God was doing in their midst; they were enthusiastic students of the Scriptures who considered every word of the sacred text infallible and yet were deaf to what God was saying to them now; and at his feet he had a woman who knew in her own life the power of God to change the world with his forgiveness! She, the outcast sinner, knew what they, the religious experts, ought to have known but did not know. On the surface and according to the accepted religious mind they were the men of God and she was the enemy of God, offensive to him because of her disregard of his law. But below the surface, if one had eyes as Jesus had to see below the surface, *they* were the enemies of God, concealing from themselves the sin of self-centeredness that made them blind to God and useless to God, and *she* was the true and faithful witness to the work of God.

Some commentators seem to assume that the woman was not forgiven until Jesus spoke the words, "Your sins are forgiven." This fastens the forgiveness of God (for it is God's forgiveness and not just Jesus' forgiveness) much too closely to a formula of words and fails to take account of the subtler ways in which forgiveness finds expression. When Jesus said to Zacchaeus, "Come down, for I am going home with you," the love of God reached out and took possession of Zacchaeus before ever Jesus said a word about forgiveness. So also here, the woman did not need to be told that she was being received with open arms into the realm to which Jesus belonged. With so much hostility surrounding her, she knew that what distinguished Jesus from all the others in the room was that he did not reject her. She was accepted. She was forgiven. She was loved. The words which were spoken later only confirmed publicly the forgiveness that had already been given and received.

It is notable that in the whole encounter as it unfolds the name of God is not mentioned. The presence of God broods over the scene but no one speaks of him. Passive tenses are used: "Her many sins have been forgiven," "where little has been forgiven," which eliminate the mention of God. This may well be deliberate, for none of the words attributed to Jesus are particularly religious. Rather, they are simply the words required to deal with the situation and with the two kinds of persons with integrity. The avoidance of any mention of God may stand in antithesis to the glibness with which the Pharisee would speak of God, always with the assumption that he and God belonged together. This would then be parallel with the restraint of Jesus in speaking of sin. It is striking that Jesus says so little about sin when his whole mission was aimed at its conquest, while, in contrast, the Pharisees busied themselves continually with men's sins but did nothing to overcome them.

The Parable

There was nothing perceptibly religious about the question posed to Simon by Jesus. We call it a parable but Simon had no way of knowing that this was a parable with a hidden meaning. So far as he was concerned it was a situation in secular life on which he was being asked to pronounce a judgment. He had no way of knowing that his relation to God and the woman's relation to God were both hidden in the story he was being told. Nor could he know that this story was God's word of judgment upon him which could become God's word of salvation for him if he had ears to hear. This was his hour of crisis. God was at his door and he did not know it. It was such a simple story. Who would expect divine judgment and salvation to arrive in such a guise? Two men in debt to a moneylender was the commonest of occurrences in any Palestinian town, one with a small debt and one with a great one. The uncommon element in the story was the generosity of the moneylender who canceled both debts when the two debtors had nothing to pay. Then came the question to which the answer seemed so obvious that one wondered why the question would be asked at all: Which of the two debtors will love his benefactor most? That is, which of them will be most grateful to him? Simon had no alternative but to give the obvious answer.

Until that moment Simon had no reason to suspect that Jesus' words had anything to do with the woman. He must have still been wondering what Jesus was getting at when suddenly Jesus, by turning to the woman, drew her into the situation. Now began the interpretation of the parable, the identification of the two debtors, the lifting of the veil that had hidden the story's meaning. Jesus did not spare his host by any false politeness. He could be ruthless where a man's or a woman's life was at stake. That was what made him either loved or hated. He simply pointed out to Simon the contrast between his own omission of the usual acts of courtesy and care for a guest and the woman's profuse expressions of love and devotion. "Can you not see," he was saying to Simon, "that this grateful love in its profusion is an indication of how great a debt has been forgiven this woman? And can you not see that that cold, discourteous heart of yours is an indication that you know nothing of the forgiving love of God?" "To whom little is forgiven, the same loveth little." Love, generous love, like the love of God that gives itself where it is not deserved, was the one great lack at the center of the Pharisee's religion. Paul knew this well and in I Cor., ch. 13, he undoubtedly has in mind both Jewish and Christian Pharisees when he pictures the religious man in all his excellence of oratory, knowledge, faith, generosity, and self-sacrifice, but through his lack of love worth nothing to God.

The depths of the parable are profound. It has in it not just Simon and the woman but all mankind. All men, if they knew the truth of their situation before God, would know themselves bankrupts with no hope except in God's forgiveness. It does not matter whether their debt, their sin, is great or small; it separates them from God, and, in separating them from God, keeps them from knowing their only true life in fellowship with God. They cannot be themselves until their sin is overcome, forgiven. The Pharisee in his scrupulous obedience to the law has so minimized his sin that he no longer lets himself be branded a sinner. Sinners are those outrageous people who flaunt the law by their conduct and whose very presence is a source of defilement. Rabbi Jehuda ben Baba on his deathbed said that there was only one sin he could remember in his lifetime. Paul, looking back on his life under the law, claimed that his record had been blameless. But where Jesus broke with the Pharisees and stood rather with the prophets was in his recognition of the involvement of all men in sin. "There is none good save God." For a man to know God is to know his distance from God and his alienation from God. Paul's emphasis in Romans upon the universality of sin and upon the self-deception of religious men in thinking that by their religious performances they can justify themselves before God is an elaboration of what Jesus says so simply in his parable. The parable also exposes the absurdity of the established line of demarcation between righteous and sinners and of the presumption of the righteous in sitting in judgment upon those whom they regarded as sinners. Bankrupts looking down on other bankrupts merely because of the difference in the size of their respective debts! The line between righteous and sinners was basic to the established order of the Jewish community and Jesus' negation of its validity was like an earthquake to those on both sides of the line.

Even though Jesus is ruthless in disclosing to Simon his true situation, he is also surprisingly gentle with him. The parable says, "Yes, Simon, I know that your sin is very small in comparison with the sin of this woman, but nevertheless it is sin and it both separates you from God and disrupts your life until you confess it frankly and find forgiveness for it." He did not draw from Simon's lovelessness the conclusion that he might well have drawn, that Simon knew nothing of God's forgiveness or love. He said only, "To whom little is forgiven, the same loveth little." With that arrow plunged into Simon's conscience he turned away from him to the woman and, even as she had made public confession of her contrition, he made public declaration of her forgiveness.

The last two verses may have been added to the story from elsewhere in its transmission (e.g., Luke 5:21; 17:19), but it must be admitted that they are appropriate in their present position. Jesus' forgiving of sins, which was the very heart of his mission, must have seemed sheer presumption if not blasphemy to men who in their strict monotheism made forgiveness the prerogative of God alone. Many Christians are closer to the Pharisees than to Jesus on this point in their failure to grasp that God's forgiveness, incarnate in a human person in Jesus, meeting broken selves with the divine love and mending them, was only the beginning of a mission that was meant to continue in all of Jesus' disciples. Jesus was the spearhead of a divine invasion of our world, God's love no longer waiting for the sinner to seek forgiveness but, indwelling human selves, going in search of the sinner to reconcile him to his God, to his own self and to his fellowman. Christians are not aware of the company they keep when they think to do honor to Jesus in saying that he alone can forgive, when his intention was that in union with him, sharing his life in God, his disciples should forgive as God forgives and, in doing so, be ministers of the same reconciliation.

The final words of Jesus to the woman, "Your faith has saved you; go in peace," are open to serious misunderstanding. We have already noted that there is no mention of the object of faith. Is it faith in Jesus, faith in God, or just faith? The danger is that because of the absence of any mention of the object of faith, the conclusion may be drawn that for Jesus faith was something which a person of himself can choose to have, an attitude in life which he can decide to adopt. But the faith of the woman is plainly her response to the forgiving love of God which met her in Jesus' dealings with her. Divine love has called forth in her a corresponding love. The barriers have been cleared away by forgiveness. God is with her and she is with God. That is the strength and joy of her faith, not something that she achieves of herself but something that is wholly the work of God in her and yet at the same time wholly her own. She is not less herself because God is with her and takes possession of her life, but rather for the first time truly and wholly herself. Jesus can tell her to go in peace because he knows that the God of peace goes with her and will abide with her forever.

Chapter III

JESUS, LEVI,
AND THE TAX COLLECTORS

THE BIBLE, read naïvely and without imagination, can create very false impressions. Some people, taking Mark 1:14–15 with complete literalness, have assumed that Jesus' preaching at the beginning of his ministry consisted of no more than fourteen words, repeated over and over. They have not the imagination to realize that these words represent the distillation of thousands of words spoken in his earliest preaching and teaching. So also in the account of the call of Levi, as in the parallel account of the call of Peter, Andrew, James and John in vs. 16–20, only the moment of decision is reported, so that it is as though men who had never seen Jesus before responded instantly when he suddenly appeared before them and said, "Follow me." The depiction of the call of disciples in John, ch. 1, manages to suggest the more extensive process that preceded discipleship. We cannot, therefore, read Luke 5:27–28 as a play by play account of the call of Levi: that Jesus one day in passing saw Levi in his tax collector's office, on the moment decided that Levi should be a disciple, spoke to him only the two words, "Follow me," whereupon Levi at once rose to his feet, left everything behind and from that moment went with Jesus wherever he went. We have no evidence to reconstruct how Jesus first met Levi, or by what stages he progressed until he became one of the Twelve, but we certainly must assume that when he left his tax office to become a full-time disciple, he was not following a stranger.

Because tax collectors in the "black or white" system of Judaism were classified as "sinners" and this term is fastened on them in the New Testament, the injustice is frequently done to them of taking for granted that all tax collectors in first-century Palestine were dishonest. The Roman system of "farming" taxes certainly offered an opportunity for dishonesty. It was convenient for the Roman Government to receive all the taxes of a district in a lump sum from one man who then could add his percentage to the tax as he apportioned it to collectors in smaller districts, who in turn added their own percentage. It was a legitimate business and a tax collector did not have to resort to dishonest practices in order to be prosperous. The very fact that he was prosperous from serving the hated Roman occupation forces was sufficient to make the intensely patriotic Jewish population despise any Jew who became a tax collector. He was no longer welcome in the synagogue or among respectable, law-abiding Jewish people. Along with all Gentiles, Hellenizers, and godless people in general, he was classified as a sinner. That some tax collectors were dishonest was sufficient to create the legend that all tax collectors were dishonest. It should be noted that in the story of Zacchaeus in Luke, ch. 19, Zacchaeus does not confess dishonesty in his former conduct but rather rejects the slur on his character. A man who has cheated *everyone* does not say, "If I have cheated anyone, I am ready to repay him four times over." Zacchaeus had no expectation of a long line of applicants waiting for a very nice profit on his defalcations! And yet the legend persists in sermons on Zacchaeus that he was an evil, dishonest man before he met Jesus. Perhaps a parallel to the way in which good, synagogue-attending people felt about tax collectors would be the way in which most good, church-attending people feel about bartenders. They would be shocked at finding a minister enjoying the companionship of bartenders (apparently more than he enjoyed the society of members of his church!) and they would be astonished at hearing that one of the bartenders had become a missionary.

It requires a considerable effort to grasp how high the wall was that divided the Jewish community into two compartments,

one for the righteous and one for the sinners. Ritual purity demanded a strict separation of the two. Only the most scrupulous
care in obeying all the regulations prescribed by the law could
qualify one for membership in the holy community. Faith in
Israel's God was equated with obedience to the complex net-
work of laws extracted from Scripture and tradition which were
taken to be the authoritative expression of the will of God.
Therefore, disobedience in regard to any part of the law or
refusal to take one's whole pattern of life from the law was
equated with faithlessness and called for the exclusion of the
offender from the synagogue, from the community of the righteous and from any claim to belong to the true Israel of God. It
was taken for granted that to be a sinner was to be abandoned
by God. Sinners had no share in the consolations of faith or in
the glorious future that awaited the true Israel. For them there
was only the wrath of God. All of God's care was for the community of the righteous. To be excluded from that community
was to be shut out from God. Only when we become aware of
the sociological and psychological consequences of this rigid
order can we understand what it meant that Jesus considered
himself "sent unto the lost sheep of the house of Israel." He was
flaunting the time-honored distinction by which the holy community protected itself against pollution, encouraging sinners
to question the judgment of the religious authorities concerning
them, and in general upsetting the established order of the Jewish
religious and social world.

THE MODERN WALL

We deceive ourselves, however, if we think that this kind of
wall has had its existence only in the Jewish community of Jesus'
day. We do not think today in terms of "righteous" and "sinners." We do not have two thousand laws which one must
observe in order to retain his place in the religious community.
But we do have an invisible wall between insiders and outsiders
which operates very effectively and has tragic consequences for
persons on both sides of the wall. Conformity to the standards

of the religious community is expected of all who would retain their place in it. Frequently, public conformity is sufficient, what the person does in private being left out of consideration. But when a man or woman publicly offends against the accepted standards, no official act of exclusion is necessary because the offender will most likely exclude himself automatically. He no longer belongs. But one may be an outsider without having committed any offense. Some are outsiders because they have grown up in families that were uninterested in the church. Some have grown up as insiders but for some reason have seceded from the church. Some are neither indifferent nor in rebellion but, having drifted away from the church for a time, feel themselves to be on the outside not knowing how to find the way back in. All such outsiders would be agreed on one point, the height of the wall that separates them from the Christian worshiping community.

From within the Christian community the wall is not so readily evident. The members of the church tend to live in a world of their own. This is particularly true of ministers who may spend the whole of their time within the circle of church families and involved in church organizations so that they are hardly aware of the existence of the world of the outsiders so close at hand. Their congregations expect them to spend their time in the spiritual care of members and adherents of the church and in directing the affairs of the institution. New members for the congregation come chiefly from the children of church families and the transfer of members from other congregations. Only a very tiny percentage comes from beyond the wall behind which the religious community has its life. Even the mass evangelistic services that are supposed to reach the outsiders have only a very small fraction of their converts from beyond the wall. Their greatest success is with lukewarm church members.

Some features of the ancient Jewish situation are reproduced in our modern division of the community religiously into insiders and outsiders. It is taken for granted that God belongs with the insiders and that Jesus is their private property. The outsider has no minister of religion who cares whether he lives or dies. The ministers and church members are too busy taking care of each other and of their institutional programs to have any time for him. They are conscious that the maintenance of moral and spiritual standards is their responsibility before God and they cannot help but feel a superior virtue in themselves in comparison with the irresponsible outsiders. This consciousness of superiority may at times issue in an arrogant self-righteousness and an attitude of harsh judgment upon those who stand outside the religious community. But, however that may be, the wall is there and those who bear the name of Jesus Christ are usually shut in behind the wall, either by the weight of their institutional duties or by their religious attitude. Therefore, Jesus' breaching of the wall is of significance not only in understanding his mission within the first-century Jewish community but in interpreting the consequences of that mission for a church that today would maintain its continuity with him.

THE MISSION BEYOND THE WALL

Had Jesus restricted his preaching and teaching to orderly occasions in the synagogue and his social intercourse to the community of the "righteous," he would have met with criticism and argument but it is doubtful whether the religious authorities would have taken him so seriously or have felt themselves so dangerously threatened by him. What offended them so deeply was his refusal to recognize the validity of the wall between the righteous and the sinners. To them it was obvious that as a religious teacher he belonged with the "righteous" in the synagogue. He had grown up in Nazareth as a faithful member of the synagogue community. The conservatism of his brother James when he became the head of the Jerusalem church suggests a family that held strictly to the Pharisaic pattern of religion. But the tradition points consistently to the frustration and hostility Jesus met in more than one synagogue as he began his mission. The "righteous" had no ears for his gospel. Soon we find him preaching on the hillside or the seashore or in someone's home. He made contact with people on the other side of the wall and among them met with a welcome such as he had never experienced in the synagogue. He found the supposedly irreligious and ungodly outsiders more ready to hear and respond to his gospel than the religious insiders. Soon the report was current that he was letting himself be entertained at dinner in the homes of tax collectors and other such disreputable people. And what hurt most was that he made no secret of the fact that he was much more at home among them than among the "righteous."

There is no indication that Jesus turned his back on the synagogue. We would understand it if he had very early declared the synagogue community to be in a hopeless state of spiritual paralysis and, breaking with it completely, had directed his mission exclusively to the outsiders. He seems rather to have carried on a twofold ministry, in the synagogue and beyond the synagogue, that is, on both sides of the wall. All Israel had to have the opportunity of hearing his gospel. Nevertheless, it has to be taken seriously that he described his "calling" or "sending" as being "to the lost sheep of the house of Israel," and that these are to be specifically identified with the Jewish community outside the wall.

This double character and double setting of Jesus' ministry would be likely to produce two quite different types of disciple. We are familiar today with how differently two people respond to the gospel when one of them comes from completely outside the religious community and at once grasps the revolutionary impact of Christian faith, while the other, from long familiarity with religious language and with what he takes to be the Christian life, is blinded to the more radical aspects of the gospel. What we hear is determined to such a degree by the context into which we receive the words. Therefore, we would expect the disciples who came from beyond the wall to be more radical Christians than those who from the beginning were saturated with Jewish religious tradition. In Acts we find some such distinction as this between the Aramaic-speaking church which retained its intensely Jewish character and managed to continue in the context of the Jewish community and the church of the

Hellenists, led by Stephen and Philip, which was more sharply critical of the established order in Judaism and more ready to launch out on a mission beyond Jerusalem and the Jewish people. Is it not possible that this church of the Hellenists is largely the product of Jesus' mission to the outsiders? Jewish outsiders would mix freely with Greek-speaking Gentiles in a way that was impossible for anyone who wished to retain his orthodox status as an insider, so that it would not be surprising for the church of the outsiders to receive the designation of the church of the Hellenists. It was from this church that Paul drew his first knowledge of the Christian movement and into whose association he was drawn after his conversion.

Adolf Schlatter,[11] followed by Rengstorf[12] in the Kittel *Theological Dictionary,* has maintained that Jesus accepted the Jewish distinction of righteous and sinners and that there is no irony in his use of the words in the present encounter. This would be a possible interpretation if one considered the passage in complete isolation. Jesus, criticized for mingling freely with sinners, i.e., for failing to preserve his religious purity in the society of the pure, would then be understood as agreeing that the members of the orthodox religious community are pure, righteous, and healthy in God's sight and that the outsiders are all of them sinners, unrighteous, impure, and unhealthy. If this were valid, then he was merely indicating to his critics politely that they needed no such ministry as his and that in mingling with sinners he was going where he was needed. But this interpretation ignores the theological content of the parable which we considered in the last chapter, in which Jesus portrayed the righteous Pharisee as a debtor before God, the smallness of whose debt did not in any way relieve him of the necessity for forgiveness or give him the right to consider himself anything except a sinner. It ignores Jesus' words to the rich young ruler, "There is none good save God." And it ignores the parable of the prodigal in which sinners and righteous are represented by the two sons, one who declared his independence of the father and one who remained obediently at home but was as alienated from his father's mind and heart as the one who removed himself to a distance. To dull the sharp edge of Jesus' affront to the righteous community is to silence his critique of man's religiousness and to open the way for the restoration of the illusion that the sincerely religious man is no longer to count himself in the full sense a sinner.

We get the full flavor of Jesus' answer to his self-righteous critics only when we recognize the irony in the words. "It is not healthy people like you who need a doctor. Why are you surprised then to find the doctor among the sick? It is not righteous people like you who need my call to repentance. Why are you surprised, then, to find me among sinners for whom that call is so appropriate?" We can conjure up the look on Jesus' face as he spoke the words. These were the men who, like the Pharisee Simon, were blind to their own sickness, unaware of how far they were from God or of how sterile they were in their self-centered religiousness. Their sickness was the absence in them of anything of the love of God. And these were the men who in the synagogue had been turning a deaf ear to Jesus' gospel, finding in it nothing that seemed to be applicable to themselves. If they had eyes to see, they would know that they were the sick and the sinners and that this man before them was the One sent from God to bring them healing for their sickness, forgiveness for their sin, and a new life in God. The irony in Jesus' words was subtle. It is doubtful whether his critics would be aware of it. To them it would seem that Jesus was according them their due respect as the righteous who needed no repentance. Only those who knew enough of Jesus' mind to know that for him self-righteousness was the very essence of sin, the most God-excluding sin of all, would detect the irony. It is quite possible that the "sinners" whose company Jesus was enjoying would see the point, and in fact were intended to see the point, of the irony immediately.

To explore the full dimensions of Jesus' mission to the outsiders, it is best perhaps to begin with his likening of himself to a shepherd sent in search of the lost sheep of the house of Israel. We can surely assume that in using this image Jesus was familiar with the thirty-fourth chapter of Ezekiel in which God, through Ezekiel, denounces the irresponsible shepherds of Israel who are more interested in using the sheep for the provision of their own food and clothing than in caring faithfully for the welfare of the flock, so that the sheep are scattered on the mountains with no shepherd. God then promises to come himself as the shepherd of the flock, to seek them out wherever they are scattered, to gather them from among the nations, to feed them, to bind up the broken, to strengthen the sick. The same image of the shepherd occurs in Second Isaiah (Isa. 40:11), with God as the shepherd who brings the scattered sheep home, but the work of gathering the scattered Israelites and restoring Israel is then assigned to the Servant of the Word (Isa., ch. 49), which is Israel in fulfillment of its God-given destiny. The Servant reflects on earth the character and purpose of God in heaven. He proclaims good news to the poor, binds up the broken-hearted, gives sight to the blind and liberty to the prisoners (Isa. 42:7; 61:1). Luke's tradition that Jesus described his mission as the fulfillment of the promise of Isa. 61:1 (Luke 4:16 ff.) is a highly credible one, and it is significant for the present discussion that in Isa. 49:5–6 the mission of the Servant is in two stages: first, the restoration of Israel, and second, the evangelization of the nations by the restored Israel. There is no sign that Jesus in his lifetime considered his or his disciples' mission as more than the fulfillment of the first stage. Certainly Peter, James, and the Jerusalem church understood their missionary commission, to preach the gospel everywhere, as a mission only to Jews scattered across the world. The recognition of this makes Paul's commission from the risen Lord himself, to take the gospel to the Gentiles, much more a crucial turning point. What Paul discerned was Jesus' intention that his Servant mission should move from the first stage to the second stage.[13] The author of Acts has obscured the clarity of the two stages in his desire to give the original apostles the credit for initiating the ministry to the Gentiles, but the letter to the Galatians leaves not a shadow of doubt that even Peter understood his commission as primarily to his own scattered Jewish people, though he could on occasion make exceptions (Gal. 2:9). It was Paul who first rightly understood that when Jesus broke out of the narrow and confining synagogue community to fulfill his mission to the Jewish outsiders, he was on his way not only to them but beyond them to the world of the Gentiles.

A parallel term to "searching for lost sheep" was "fishing for men" and it is important to note that Jesus' interest in making disciples was to enlist them and train them to participate with him in his search (|| fishing). His aim was not to get the outsiders back into the synagogue and make them good orthodox, synagogue-supporting Jews like the ones already there, but to engage all who responded to his gospel in a mission which would accomplish for Israel what the synagogue had failed to do. This may have important implications for the church's understanding of evangelism which is so often focused on making outsiders into insiders who then are so spiritually comfortable as insiders that they forget there is any need for a mission to outsiders. Jesus recognized that his whole purpose would be defeated if he did nothing more than restore to the synagogue a number of its lapsed members. The restoration of Israel meant the creation of a new Israel, and he saw more hope of its birth among the outsiders than from the synagogue community. What was needed was not a return to the synagogue but a return to the living God with whatever consequences that might have for the whole community. And yet he did not desert the synagogue. He remained a worshiper in it and continued to preach in it. After all, in his evaluation of Israel the righteous citizens in the synagogue were lost sheep too, merely of a different kind from the ones outside. Like Stephen and Paul and Luther, he remained in the religious institution into which he had been born until he was expelled from it by his crucifixion. He was no facile innovator. When he met frustration in the synagogue he did not leave it and establish a new place of worship for himself. But neither did he let himself be restrained by it from going forward with his mission in his own way.

He was fisherman, shepherd, and now he added a third image to describe his mission—physician. This has a profound significance, particularly in contrast to the attitude of Pharisees toward their fellowmen. For them sin was not a sickness but a willful disobedience to the law of God for which the sinner must be held strictly to account both before God and by the people of God whose very existence was defiled and endangered by the sin of any Israelite. Loyalty to God and to Israel demanded an attitude of severity and exclusion toward every sinner. The only solution to the problem of sin was for the sinner to repent of it, seek forgiveness from God, and commit himself to the strictest conformity to the law. The sign of a true repentance would be an exemplary keeping of the law which would then qualify the person for restoration to the orthodox worshiping community. The whole problem of sin was dealt with on a superficial level as though it were nothing more than a matter of regulating one's conduct. Jesus, in contrast to this, went to the very heart of man's problem with himself when he defined sin as sickness. With Gen., ch. 3, and Ps. 51, he understood sin as the pretentiousness of man's self in making itself the center of its world, thereby disrupting the relation with God, and he knew that, as long as man was without God at the center of his life, he could neither be truly himself nor have a healthful relationship with his fellowmen. Man could be man only in a relation with God in which the love and truth and mercy of God would be reflected in his human existence. But that relation could come into being only on God's initiative.

First, then, the love of God, the mercy of God, the truth of God, had to go in search of men who in their brokenness and blindness did not know any longer what their life could and should be. It was not sufficient like John the Baptist to issue a call to repentance and wait in the wilderness for men to come and, repenting, find forgiveness. The forgiveness had to take human form and go up and down the roads of Palestine seeking men and women who in their helplessness did not know that forgiveness was possible. The sickness of sin was the dividedness of men within themselves that alienated them from God and from their fellowmen. The cure was the forgiveness of God that restored a man to his true, original life in God, responding to God's love with a love like his own. Therefore in setting forgiveness at the center of his mission Jesus could depict himself as a physician whose duty it was to go wherever men acknowledged themselves to be suffering from the sickness of sin. But he did not choose to be alone in his doctoring. He enlisted disciples to share his task with him, and it was essential to their equipment that the same infinitely forgiving love of God which was his life should also be their life.

Jesus was criticized not only for being with the tax collectors but also for eating and drinking with them. This criticism had two prongs. To eat and drink with sinners who would be neglectful of the Jewish food laws would be to make himself unclean, but Luke 5:33–35, which is a continuation of Luke 5:27–32, reports the accusation that Jesus in his evident enjoyment of food and drink in Levi's house was showing himself to be a less godly man than John the Baptist, who engaged frequently in fasts and taught his disciples to do the same. Jesus' answer to the accusation combines seriousness with playfulness, an ironic playfulness that is in keeping with the spirit of vs. 31–32. "Surely you do not expect the guests at a wedding feast to fast!" No occasion in Jewish life was more joyful than a wedding. All laws concerning fasting were suspended for it. But what was a union of man and wife in comparison with a reunion of man with God? The same joyful note is struck in the parable of the prodigal's return in which the exuberance of the celebration instituted by the Father serves as a justification of Jesus' own joyful celebration of the return of such prodigals as Levi. Joy was the keynote of Jesus' mission in contrast to the more plodding character of Pharisaic religion and the asceticism of John the Baptist. To be sons of God the Father was to be at home in the Father's world and to receive with gratitude all that God had provided for his family. Jesus' enjoyment of food and drink was an essential expression of one aspect of his gospel. To be restored to one's life in God was, as the beatitudes say plainly, to inherit the earth, to enter into the true possession of all things in the world, to know the joy of having each moment of one's present life in the world transformed by the coming of God's Kingdom.

A church that professes to be the body in which Jesus is continuing his mission in the modern world may well be disturbed by this story, by the astonishing similarities between itself and the orthodox synagogue community, the insiders, and also by its equally astonishing failure, in most of its projects for the evangelizing of the outsiders, to let itself be guided by Jesus' example in his initial mission to the lost sheep of the house of Israel.

Chapter IV

JESUS AND THE EXPERT THEOLOGIAN

THE USE OF THE TERM "LAWYER" conceals the real nature of the encounter in Luke 10:25–37 which drew forth from Jesus the parable of the good Samaritan. In Judaism, civil and religious laws were mingled together and the whole duty of man was scrupulous obedience to the law in its every detail. The ordinary man, therefore, required the help of an expert in the law to define for him exactly what was permitted and what was not permitted. Today we would call such an expert not a lawyer but a theologian with ethics as his specialty. The encounter, thus, is between Jesus and a theologian whose task is the careful definition of what every Israelite must do in order to be well-pleasing to God.

First, however, we must establish that the dialogue between Jesus and the theologian and the parable belong together, since it is questioned by some scholars.[14] Bultmann in his *History of the Synoptic Tradition*[15] takes for granted that the dialogue is a Lucan reshaping of the encounter reported in Mark 12:28–34, the original well-intentioned representative of Judaism being transformed into a hostile questioner and the incident being used as a setting for Jesus' parable. B. T. D. Smith in *The Parables of the Synoptic Gospels*[16] separates the parable from the setting on the grounds that it does not answer the question which was asked, that to the question, Who is my neighbor? Jesus responds by describing what it means to be a neighbor. But Smith does not consider the possibility that Jesus may be looking past the formal question to the vital life-or-death question of this man's existence so that the seeming incongruity of the answer with the question is intrinsic to Jesus' way of dealing with men. Gilmour in *The Interpreter's Bible*[17] finds Luke's omission of the Marcan story convincing evidence that Luke constructed the setting for the parable by revising Mark's material, and he follows Smith in seeing an incongruity between the question and the answer. But the absence of the Marcan story in Luke can as well be explained as the result of Luke's having in his traditions an account of this much more vivid and striking encounter. Actually, the Marcan and Lucan accounts have little more in common than the summarizing of the law in the two great commandments. In Mark, Jesus makes the summary and the scribe agrees, whereas in Luke, Jesus elicits the summary from the scribe. But in Mark the scribe receives Jesus' commendation, whereas in Luke he is the subject of incisive criticism. Since Jesus must have had encounters with different types of such scribes or theologians, there is no strong reason to assume that both accounts are versions of the same story. The unity of the setting with the parable, however, becomes most convincing when the unique function of the parable in relation to this kind of person is grasped.

This parable, like some others, has suffered frequently from the application to it of an inadequate concept of parable. The idea has been widespread that all of Jesus' parables should be subject to a single definition when actually they vary rather widely in character. George A. Buttrick[18] in 1930 asserted that in his estimation the orthodox description of a parable as "an earthly story with a heavenly meaning" could hardly be improved on. Adolf Jülicher, whose work[19] in this field has long been regarded as a classic, defined the narrative parables as illustrative instances which establish an abstract religious or ethical truth by the evidence of a concrete case. One book of sermons on the parables actually entitled them *Little Stories of Jesus* and treated them as illustrations of moral and religious truths. As a consequence of such interpretation the content of the parable of the good Samaritan is reduced to the platitude, "Be kind to people in trouble," and the parable of the talents to,

"Be sure to use your talents however small they are." The meaning of each can be read off the surface without the slightest difficulty. In fact, they are understood as simplifications and objectifications of obvious truths. There should have been a warning against this way of thinking in Jesus' description of the parable as a method of concealing the truth (Mark 4:10–12). This, however, has usually been dismissed as a product of the church's misunderstanding of the function of the parable and its tendency to make mysterious what was actually plain and simple.

More attention to the prophets' use of parables in the Old Testament would have provided a more adequate approach. One attempt in this direction was made by A. T. Cadoux in his *Parables of Jesus*. He attacked the concept of them "as inculcating a commonplace of morals or religion" and asserted as their function "to help home a resented, distasteful, or, at least, difficult truth. In its most pointed use, as in Nathan's parable to David, or Jesus' parable to Simon the Pharisee, it brings the hearer to self-condemnation before he sees where he is being led."[20] The parables "gain in value when we see them, not as pictorial renderings of accepted truths, but as moments in the creative reaction of Jesus upon the life around him. They take us into the brunt of his warfare."[21] But this insight needs to be carried much farther than it was taken by Cadoux. We need to see how the parable in the hands of prophets was a device for laying men open to God's judgment upon them, a sword of the Spirit which cut so deeply through men's spiritual defenses that it left them naked before God, and that Jesus, standing in the prophetic tradition, perfected this type of parable.

THE PARABLE IN THE OLD TESTAMENT

Nathan's parable before King David in II Sam., ch. 12, forms an admirable starting point. David had used his position of power to satisfy an illicit passion. He desired another man's wife for himself and it was a simple matter to arrange that the other man, a foreigner, Uriah, should be placed in the front line of battle. Someone had to be in the front line and absorb the first shock of the enemy. Since someone had to die for the nation, it was convenient that it should be Uriah. It was all done so quietly that David deceived even himself as to the real nature of his act. It was a heartless murder. But he did not deceive the prophet Nathan. The keen eyes of the prophet missed nothing where justice in Israel was concerned. Appearing before the king, Nathan told a pitiful story of a poor man wronged. He pictured the poverty-stricken little home where a pet lamb was the only comfort and joy of father and children. Then, like a tornado, into the touching scene comes the wealthy neighbor who seizes and kills the poor man's pet lamb to make a feast for a guest, instead of using one out of his own great flock of sheep. David's whole soul revolted at once at the tale of callous cruelty. His anger blazed out and he vowed that such a man had forfeited his right to live. As king he pronounced sentence of death upon him. Then, suddenly, he became aware that Nathan's finger was pointed at him and Nathan was saying: "Thou art the man!"

How could anyone call Nathan's parable "an earthly story with a heavenly meaning" or an illustration of moral or religious truth and think thereby to have defined it? It was a clever trap that Nathan used to get David into a helpless and defenseless position where the truth would really strike home to him. It was part of a breathless game that the prophet played, with a human soul and his own life for the stakes. It was a sharp sword with which he cut through the iron bonds of self-deception and made a man see himself as he really was before the face of God. The intention of the parable is not moral or religious teaching but revelation and redemption, to bring a man under the judgment of God and strike from his eyes the blindness to himself that threatens to be his ruin. Its content is not an abstract truth but rather the truth of a man's existence. Moreover, that truth is *hidden, secreted,* in a simple story until the hearer discovers in it God's word of judgment upon him, a judgment that may lead him to repentance and make possible his redemption. This prophetic device builds upon the fact that human beings see and condemn quickly in others the very faults to which they are quite blind when they are present in themselves. The human conscience works with a remarkable efficiency and sensitivity when the case presented to it does not involve in any way the person who has been asked to judge. But the same conscience, turned upon ourselves, at once is afflicted with peculiar blindnesses. It was to outwit this fatal quirk in human nature that the prophets originated and Jesus perfected this cunning parabolic device.

The presence in the Old Testament of four more instances of this device and its use on a number of occasions by Jesus is sufficient justification for considering it an independent and consciously developed type in the general field of parable.

A second example occurs in II Sam., ch. 14, where it is narrated that Joab secured the services of a "wise woman" from Tekoa to act out a parable before David. The purpose in this instance was to change David's attitudes toward his son Absalom, but the technique was the same. David was led to pronounce a merciful judgment upon the surviving son of a woman whose two sons had quarreled and one had slain the other in the quarrel. The woman then applied this judgment to his own relation to Absalom who had been banished for the killing of his brother.

Again, in I Kings 20:35–43, an unnamed prophet, taking serious exception to Ahab's merciful conduct toward the Syrian, Ben-hadad, used a parable in order to accuse the king of a breach of trust in letting Ben-hadad go. He himself acted the part of a soldier who, having been entrusted with a prisoner, was in peril of his life for having permitted the prisoner to escape. Ahab fell readily into the trap, gave judgment, and in a moment was made to realize that he had actually passed judgment upon himself.

Isaiah's parable of the vineyard in Isa. 5:1–6 shows the same technique in addressing a larger audience. The hearers would be familiar from their own experience or from observation with the problems in establishing a fruitful vineyard. As Isaiah in his poem depicted his friend's experience with his vineyard, they would follow the story with real sympathy. The vintner chose a fruitful hill, fenced it properly and cleared it of stones. He planted in it only the choicest vines. Yet in spite of all his care it produced only useless wild grapes. The audience was asked, then, to say what should be done to such a vineyard. They knew what should be done. The fruitless vineyard should be broken down and abandoned so that no one would any longer waste his time and money on it. At this point Isaiah tore open the parable and let his audience know that they had pronounced judgment upon themselves and upon the whole house of Israel. They were God's vineyard and all his care had been wasted upon them.

The Book of Jonah is a magnificent example of this type of parable. The situation faced by the prophetic author was an ever-narrowing nationalism in the religion of his people. They were unwilling to see in the nations beyond Israel anything but fuel for the fires of Yahweh's wrath. The destiny promised to the posterity of Abraham—that they would be a source of blessing to all the nations (Gen. 12:2)—no longer interested them. The vision of Second Isaiah of a day when all men would bow the knee to the God of Israel and join with Israelites in his service had been allowed to fade. In order to cut through such blindness and prejudice, the author of The Book of Jonah laid hold of the prophet's sharpest weapon, the parable that under pretense of telling a story would strip bare the soul of the nation. But this author had also a delicate sense of humor and he used it to reduce the standpoint of his people to an absurdity. Sometimes gentle and playful ridicule can be more powerful than mighty arguments. As the history of Jonah was unfolded, nationalistic Jews would follow his course with sympathy. They, too, if commanded by God to go and preach repentance to godless Assyrians in Nineveh, would take ship in the opposite direction for Spain. They would not cooperate even with God to save the Assyrians from their well-merited destruction. And yet they would agree also that Jonah did the right and noble thing in letting himself be cast overboard from the ship that the poor heathen sailors might not lose their lives through his disobedience to God. In a specific situation in contact with non-Jews they themselves would not be lacking in compassion. But in giving this agreement they fell into the cleverly prepared trap. Jonah can be merciful to foreigners and they can be merciful to foreigners, but God must not be merciful to them!

The author had in his story a second hook on which to catch his narrow-minded fellow countrymen. In ch. 4, Jonah, having preached to Nineveh and seen the remarkable repentance of the population, sits down outside the city to see what will happen, hoping that it may yet be destroyed and sorrowing at the prospect that God may be moved to compassion by the repentance. The miraculous gourd grows up to shade the prophet from the sun but, just as quickly, it dies when a worm attacks it. Jonah is provoked at the death of the gourd. He has pity for the gourd, but he is unwilling that God should have pity on the people and cattle of Nineveh! The story is a mirror held up to the nation that they may see their own faces in it and recognize the absurdity of such an attitude in Israel, the people of a God whose nature is compassion.

THE PARABLE IN ITS ORIGINAL SETTING

We have already in Chapter II considered one instance of Jesus' use of this prophetic parable, the parable of the two debtors which so perfectly mirrored the situation before God of the two people with whom Jesus was dealing. When we recognize the same type of parable in Luke 10:25 ff., we see at once not only that the parable and the setting belong inseparably to each other but also that the parable had a very different meaning in its original setting than is usually attributed to it. There is one meaning that can be read off the surface when it is isolated, but there is another sharper message hidden in it for persons who, like the lawyer, have come to consider themselves experts in the field of religion.

The whole tone of the encounter is set by the statement that the lawyer in asking his question was putting Jesus to the test. He is not to be conceived as an earnest inquirer, troubled by an uncertainty about life after death, who hopes to learn from Jesus the one thing necessary. Rather, he is the expert in religious questions and, to him, Jesus is the neophyte, the amateur theologian and teacher, whose competence needs to be tested. The lawyer's attitude is that of a superior to an inferior, of a teacher to a pupil. It may be that he had heard something of Jesus' teachings and had been given reason to suspect that Jesus was not as orthodox as he should be. Only when we rightly grasp this original relation between the two do we see the significance of Jesus' tactic in drawing from the questioner the answer to his own question. Jesus for the moment adopted an attitude of deference to him as the expert in the law. It was as though he said, "Come now, we all know that you are the man who is more learned in the law then any of us. Tell us what the law says and we will listen." For the moment the lawyer forgot that he had asked his question in order to test Jesus and, only too willing to display his knowledge, gave the summary of the law in the two great commandments. (It is noteworthy that this summary did not originate with Jesus but was familiar to the theologians of his day, and to the lawyer was the orthodox answer to his question. But it had a different and more radical significance for Jesus than for his contemporaries. For them it was only a summary and had to be maintained in the context of the whole complex of rabbinic law while, for Jesus, to love God and neighbor was in itself the fulfillment of all that God asked of man.)

But now the subtlety of Jesus' management of the encounter begins to appear. Having led the man on to answer his own question, Jesus dropped his attitude of deference and assumed that of a teacher with a pupil who has given the right answer: "You have answered right." The relation of the two to each other was now reversed. Jesus was pronouncing judgment on the correctness of the lawyer's knowledge. The tester was now the one who had let himself be tested. In short, he had made a bit of a fool of himself before the audience. What added to the embarrassment was Jesus' comment, "Do this and you will live." The barb in those words escapes us until we realize that the lawyer was the kind of man whose religious concern was concentrated upon refinements of definition. His doctrines had to be correct in every detail. But he was very little concerned with the translation of the doctrines into action. He would talk all day about loving God and neighbor without ever in any situation showing love for God or neighbor. He would define who his neighbor was with the most scrupulous exactness but he would never be a neighbor to any man. His religion was bottled up in intellectual definitions. Jesus recognized this and was needling him when he said, "Do this and you will live." Eternal life was not to be attained by knowing the two great commandments but only by responding in action to God and neighbor with a love that would be a reflection of God's own love to man. It should be noted that Jesus' final words to the lawyer following the parable have this same emphasis on action, "Go and do likewise." He was aware that the sickness of this man's religion was that it never issued in action.

What begins to appear now is that the parable as it was first spoken was not intended to be just an encouragement to charitable conduct in relation to the people who lie suffering and helpless at the roadside in life and that, when no more than that is found in the parable, its primary message remains unheard. It was meant originally to blast through the callous religious hide of a man who thought that by the correctness of his religious doctrines and of his religious conduct he could make himself acceptable to God. The parable is an attack on all religion that exhausts itself in forms and does nothing in the everyday world about the tragic plight of man. But, detached from its setting and erected into a kind of banner for the church's charitable enterprises, it ceases to be disturbing to us in our religiousness. Its positive encouragement of charity is separated from its ruthless critique and negation of professional piety. But once more it becomes clear that the positive element in Jesus' words, separated from the negative and critical element, is transformed into a harmless platitude. We have always to see not only what he is for but also what he is against. A "Yes" to a seemingly positive truth is valueless and empty unless at the same time we say, "No," to whatever in our immediate situation and in ourselves resists that truth.

That the lawyer was conscious that the conversation had taken a turn embarrassing to him is evident from his desire "to justify himself." He needed to demonstrate both his expertness in the law and his superiority to Jesus. He therefore asked a second question, "Who is my neighbor?" Jeremias in his *Parables of Jesus* has pointed out that the definition of neighbor was quite complex in rabbinic teaching. The problem for the rabbis was where to draw the line, who to include as the neighbors who were to be loved and treated with kindness. Heretics, informers, renegades, and all who lived in disregard of the orthodox law were excluded from the category of neighbor. Certainly the Samaritans would not have been considered neighbors. Undoubtedly the lawyer expected that he would have opportunity to give a careful detailed definition of neighbor which would demonstrate his competence. But Jesus gave him no second chance to display his knowledge. It was time to strike home to this man and the weapon that might pierce his armor of self-justification was the prophetic parable.

If our interpretation is valid, that we have here the actual setting in which the parable originated, we suddenly realize the astonishing fact that this parable, which as a literary creation has the perfection of a poem in which every word is in its only possible place, was uttered on the spur of the moment to meet a concrete situation. It was not fashioned in hours of meditation and polished over a long period of time, and yet its phrases are like the facets of a diamond. Called forth by an immediate situation that has to be understood in the context of first-century Judaism, it not only spoke with incisive relevance to that situation but has continued to speak powerfully ever since. It says a great deal to us about Jesus as a human person that in that moment he brought forth this parable and that this was his way of dealing with a man whose whole religious attitude was in antithesis to the gospel. He did not turn from him in repugnance, nor did he try to dissolve the tension between them by polite and friendly conversation. As servant of the word of God that judges and redeems he dealt faithfully and therefore ruthlessly with the problem of the man's existence before God. He used cunning to puncture his overblown self-esteem. He made no attempt to lecture him. The only way he might reach him was by hiding him away in a parable and hoping that when the parable came open to him, it would be nothing less than a laying open of his whole existence before God.

THE PARABLE ITSELF

It was essential to such a parable that the hearer should not immediately recognize himself in it. David was not told a story about a king. The lawyer-theologian was not told a story about a lawyer-theologian. He was hidden in the figures of the priest and the Levite. They were the religious experts, the professionals, men who were devoting their lives to religion. On their journey between Jerusalem and Jericho they were in a great hurry, so great that they had no time for a man lying helpless at the roadside, naked and bleeding, where robbers had left him. It has been suggested that their "passing by on the other side of the road," that is, as far from the victim as they could get as they passed, was due to their fear of being made unfit for their duties in the Temple by coming too near to what might be a dead body. There was a Sadducean rule to this effect, though the Pharisees differed on this point. The proximity of a corpse made priests and Levites unclean until they had gone through a process of ritual purification. Jesus therefore is picturing men who are so concerned about their ritual purity and their official religious duties that they close their eyes to the neighbor whom God commands them to love and leave him to die at the side of the road. Their obedience to one set of laws which they assert to be laws of God leads them to disregard the central concern of God for the poor, the broken, the naked, the helpless. There is a touch of biting satire in Jesus' representation of the priest and

Levite: they are so anxious to obey every detail of the law that they cannot even come near to their neighbor in his hour of need to discover whether he is alive or dead.

Jesus' deliberate intention of being offensive is evident in his choice of a Samaritan to do for the injured man what the priest and Levite failed to do. Some interpreters have questioned whether the Samaritan is original to Jesus' parable. They doubt whether Jesus would have represented a Samaritan as traveling regularly that piece of Jewish road and they point to Luke's particular interest in Samaritans as an indication of how a Samaritan came to be introduced at a later date into the story. But when we appreciate how determined Jesus was to shock his self-assured questioner out of his paralyzing orthodoxy, we recognize the presence of the Samaritan in the story as just the kind of aggravating twist that Jesus himself would give it. No orthodox Jew would be willing to recognize any Samaritan as his neighbor. The antipathy between Jew and Samaritan was of long standing. From the beginning of Israel's settlement in Palestine there was tension between the northern and southern tribes. Their union under David and Solomon was none too stable and soon dissolved. The two Kingdoms were rivals and sometimes enemies. Then, after the fall of the Northern Kingdom in 722 B.C. and the settlement of foreigners in the north, the Judeans began to regard their northern brothers as half-breeds. In the postexilic period when attempts were being made to rebuild the Judean community and Jerusalem, the northern district centered in Samaria saw a threat to its own welfare in the restoration of Jerusalem and opposed the reconstruction. These Samaritans considered themselves the continuation of north Israel and centered their religion in their own version of the Pentateuch. But to the Judeans they were heretics, pagans posing as true Israelites, and persons to be shunned and avoided by every means. A Jew traveling from Jerusalem to Galilee would travel a long road through the region beyond the Jordan in order to escape contact with Samaritans. The bitterness of these antipathies was intensified in Jesus' day by an action of Samaritans somewhere between A.D. 6 and 9 in defiling the Jerusalem Temple court by strewing in it dead men's bones. The nearest one can come to catching the flavor of the parable in mid-twentieth-century America would be to translate it, "But a Russian Communist, as he journeyed, came to where he was; and when he saw him, he had compassion."

By making a Samaritan the man who showed himself a true neighbor, Jesus was saying to the lawyer and to all who heard him, "Here is a man who according to your way of thinking has not the right doctrine at all and does not live according to the right version of the law of God. He is a heretic and as such an enemy not only of Israel but also of God according to your way of thinking. But on the road to Jericho he does what God wants done and he does it because the love of God that will not look unmoved on human suffering rules his heart. Take your choice now. Who stands with God, the man who scrupulously obeys a multitude of laws but has no care for the man at the roadside, or the despised heretic and outsider who cannot pass a man by in his need?" The Samaritan thus strikes a blow at the narrow legalistic orthodoxy that was so distasteful to Jesus. But he is also a breaching of the wall of Jewish nationalism. Jesus was well aware that in making it a Samaritan who really obeyed God's law to love his neighbor as himself, he was indicating that God might find his true believers beyond the bounds of the Jewish people.

The generosity of the Samaritan's neighborliness was undoubtedly meant by Jesus to stand in contrast to the legalistic calculating spirit of the lawyer as well as to the heartlessness of the priest and Levite. He did not give the man first aid and then pass on. After tending his wounds, he hoisted him onto the animal he himself had been riding, took him to the nearest inn and entrusted him to the innkeeper, promising when next he came that way to meet whatever expenditures were necessary beyond the two denarii he gave him. One cannot avoid the feeling that Jesus' emphasis on the uncalculating quality of the Samaritan's generosity is in each detail a rebuke to the lawyer's ignorance of what it means to be a neighbor to anyone except his religious colleagues. But it is also an exposition for all time of what happens to a man when the love of God takes possession of him. The difference of nationality and the centuries-old antagonism between Samaritan and Jew are forgotten. That the temples where the two men worship are rivals is no longer of any significance. Love sees only a brother man in trouble and allows no considerations of any kind to impede its action.

Having told his story, Jesus called upon the lawyer to give his judgment upon who was neighbor to the man who fell among the thieves. There was no longer any way of escape. Only one answer could be given and the lawyer gave it. No praise is due him for right judgment. No one could in that situation give any other answer. The significant thing is that in giving his judgment he had pronounced judgment upon himself. But whether or not he knew it we cannot tell. Jesus' final words, "Go and do likewise," are definitely abrupt and biting. They correspond to Nathan's, "Thou art the man." It is as though Jesus had said, "Quit trying to define who is your neighbor and go, be a neighbor to someone who needs you."

We commented earlier on the incongruity of the answer that Jesus gave when the lawyer asked him, "Who is my neighbor?" telling him instead how to be a neighbor, and we pointed out that because of this seeming incongruity a number of commentaries detach the parable from its setting. But what we should see in this, rather, is an example of Jesus' pastoral technique. He heard the man's question but at the same time he heard another deeper and more important question being asked by the man's actual existence in relation to God and neighbor. Therefore, he disregarded the surface question in order to get at the actual problem of this man's life. We note also a severity in Jesus' dealing with him, like the severity of the surgeon who cannot be too much concerned whether or not it hurts the patient when he is trying to correct a condition that endangers the patient's life. It is instructive that Jesus used a certain cunning in order to get through the man's defenses. He led him to expose himself and thereby make himself more vulnerable. But it was done not to humiliate an opponent but to lay him open to a work of grace. We are reminded of Jesus' words about being wise as serpents but harmless as doves. This cunning, this leading of a man on to expose himself, this setting of a trap from which the man will be unable to escape, is not exactly how we usually conceive Jesus' approach to men and his dealings with them. But, now that we have seen it clearly in this one instance and partially in Jesus' encounter with Simon the Pharisee, it may help us to read with fresh eyes the puzzling story of Jesus and his disciples in their encounter with the Canaanite woman.

Chapter V

JESUS, THE CANAANITE WOMAN, AND THE DISCIPLES

THE STORY OF JESUS' ENCOUNTER with the Canaanite woman in Matt. 15:21–28 has long been a source of perplexity and embarrassment to Christians. The attitude of Jesus throughout the incident is so very different from all that we would expect of him. Openness and responsiveness to men and women in their need is so constantly characteristic of him that we are shocked to find him apparently turning a woman away rudely when she seeks liberation for her demon-possessed daughter. We are still more deeply shocked when he seems to give as his reason for excluding her from his help that she does not belong racially to the Jewish people. And when he goes one step beyond this and puts her and her Gentile compatriots in the category of dogs in comparison with the Jewish children of God, he seems for the moment to have allied himself with the crudest version of nationalistic bigotry. Three times he rejected the woman, each time with increasing harshness. First, he was merely silent to her plea; then he asserted that his ministry was to Jews alone; and finally, there was the crushing remark that it was unfair to give to dogs the bread intended for the children. All that saves the situation is that after treating the woman with such rudeness, Jesus turns completely about, praises the woman's faith and does for her what she desires. But that makes his earlier conduct all the more puzzling.

Futile attempts have been made by some commentators in the past to soften the harshness of Jesus' words or to justify him in his behavior toward the woman. It has been asserted (by Origen, by Theodore of Mopsuestia, and more recently by Ernst Lohmeyer) that the word which Jesus uses for "dogs" is a diminutive and therefore denotes household pets, but in Hebrew usage and in the East in general it was never complimentary to call a person any kind of dog, and the Jewish attitude to Gentiles was so depreciatory that no one would consider it merely playful to classify Gentiles with dogs, even pet dogs. A. D. Bruce[22] in the *Expositor's New Testament* explained Jesus' words as "playful, humorous, bantering in tone," but we would have to call it a very heavy-handed and clumsy form of humor. A. H. McNeile[23] in his commentary on Matthew's Gospel is "sure that a tenderness of manner would deprive them [the words of rejection] of all their sting." But that leaves unexplained why three times over Jesus seemed to reject the woman's plea.

The commonest justification of Jesus' behavior has been to say that he was making trial of the woman's faith. He was forcing her to be like the importunate widow who, by persisting in her appeals to the unjust judge, finally moved him to grant her request. But it was not like Jesus to adopt the stance of the unjust judge or to play with a woman of faith in her hour of need merely to test the strength of her faith. It is revolting to think that he did it here. He was not elsewhere so lacking in discernment that he had to conjure up elaborate tests in order to discover the quality of a person's faith.

Another suggestion has it that Jesus' initial silence was due to an uncertainty in his own mind as to what he should do in this situation, confronted by a Gentile woman. Johannes Weiss seems to have originated this line of interpretation, representing Jesus as engaged in internal debate whether he should confine his mission to Jews alone or should allow his compassion to override the limits that he has thus far observed. Klostermann[24] and Branscomb[25] follow this lead and see the incident as marking a new stage in Jesus' understanding of his own mission and significant, therefore, of a development in Jesus himself from Jewish exclusiveness toward a more universal outlook. Both Bruce and McNeile interpret the sudden shift in Jesus' attitude as an expression of uncertainty. Bruce says, "There was probably a mixture of feelings in Christ's mind at this time; an aversion to recommence just then a healing ministry at all—a craving for rest and retirement; a disinclination to be drawn into a ministry among a heathen people which would mar the unity of his career as a prophet of God to Israel." The attempt to find an excuse for Jesus' contradictory words in this way makes of him a rather shabby kind of prophet. He is tired and does not want to get himself involved in a new ministry to Gentiles! He is concerned about the unity of his career as a prophet of God to Israel and does not want to mar it by ministering to a Gentile woman's need even though she has all the marks of a genuine faith! McNeile thinks that v. 26 may represent a continuation of Jesus' mental struggle, that he was saying to himself, "Dare I take the children's bread and cast it unto dogs?" But this assumes that until now Jesus, in limiting his mission, has been far below the level of the Old Testament prophets in his conception of the relation of the Gentiles to God, that in fact he has thought of them not as children of God but in the category of dogs!

THE TWO VERSIONS OF THE STORY

The preservation of the tradition in two quite different forms furnishes us with the problem of determining which account brings us closest to the original incident and which bears most clearly the marks of basic revision. Here we must distinguish between editorial changes and a basic revision that for some reason changes the thrust of the story. The account in Matthew is much the more highly dramatic. In Mark there is no sustained dialogue between Jesus and the foreign woman and the disciples do not come into the picture at all. The woman makes her plea on behalf of her daughter; Jesus repulses her momentarily with the assertion that it is not fair to take the children's bread and give it to dogs, and, on receiving her humble reply, grants her request. It is a fairly simple story of exorcism with only the one puzzling feature: why Jesus would for no apparent reason meet such a woman's request with what could only sound like a crude expression of Jewish religious arrogance and exclusiveness. But in Matthew the exorcism is secondary to a complex dialogue in which both the disciples and the woman are involved. It is not a simple "one to one" situation as in Mark but rather Jesus is dealing at one and the same time both with the woman and with his disciples. Also, Jesus' responses are more complex. He remains silent when the woman first makes her plea and the disciples are allowed to express their Jewish exclusiveness and their insensitiveness to the need of a foreigner. Words expressing rejection come first of all not from Jesus but from his disciples. Thus, when Jesus answers the woman, "I was sent only to the lost sheep of the house of Israel," he is doing only what his disciples asked him to do. The question is open whether in this and in the next "hard saying" he is giving voice to his own mind or to their minds. Also, in Matthew the emphasis is upon the woman's faith rather than upon the exorcism and upon Jesus' joy in discovering such faith beyond Israel in a Gentile woman. Here alone he exclaims, "O woman, great is thy faith!"

Bultmann, applying his principles of form criticism in *The History of the Synoptic Tradition,* rules that the simple story must be the original and the more complex one a later elaboration. But this principle applied ruthlessly would suggest that all complex stories must be later elaborations of original simple incidents. It leaves out of account the possibility that a tradition such as the Matthean one, which has in it some very puzzling and distressing elements, might undergo a process of simplification for that very reason. Certainly it must be admitted that the Marcan story presents a much less embarrassing picture of Jesus: there is no moment of hesitation in his response to the woman's plea and his seemingly harsh words can be understood as merely tearing from her a delightful expression of complete humility. Jesus' threefold resistance to her plea is gone and with its removal the story becomes much more acceptable in a church populated largely with Gentiles. But is it so easy to explain why anyone in any part of the first-century church would want to expand the story in order to make Jesus' resistance to a Gentile woman so much more emphatic? Certainly no Jewish Christian would be inclined to play up the greatness of the faith of a Gentile, and it is doubtful if enthusiasts for the Gentile mission would be likely to produce this exaggeration of Jesus' seeming unwillingness to recognize the need of a Gentile woman. It is really impossible to imagine a situation in the first-century church which would motivate the expansion of the story. We have also to invent a literary genius who has been able to construct a complex dramatic dialogue out of a very simple one. It is perhaps more reasonable to conclude, as B. H. Streeter[26] did in 1924, that the tradition in Matthew is closer to the original situation than that in Mark.

There are a number of instances of similar complex dialogues where Jesus is involved on two sides at once in a single conversation, and where no one would think of regarding the accounts as later elaborations of simpler stories. We have already considered two such dialogues, one in Luke 7:36–50 where Jesus' parable strikes in two directions at once, bringing the Pharisee under judgment and assuring the woman of forgiveness, and one in Luke 5:27–32 where the same words convey very different meanings to Jesus' tax-collector friends and to his religious critics. But other parables such as that of the prodigal and that of the Pharisee and the publican have the same two-edged character, cutting two ways at once. In fact, these parables establish it as a practice of Jesus to speak in such a way that his words would have this two-edged character and would do a double work for him when he found himself in a situation between two contrary attitudes. Therefore, we have only to grant the possibility of a situation in which Jesus would be confronted with a Gentile woman ready to put an unbounded faith in him and at the same time with the problem of a rude Jewish exclusiveness in his own disciples to see in Matthew's story an example of Jesus' mind operating in exactly the same way as it does in three different parables. This would suggest that the Matthean tradition takes us very close to an original encounter of Jesus which became embarrassing to the church as its original significance was forgotten so that it was reduced to the simpler Marcan form.

THE PROBLEM OF EXCLUSIVENESS IN THE EARLY CHURCH

Form criticism has made us familiar with the principle that traditions owed their preservation not to any purely historical interest but to the church's discovery in them of a relevance to its own problems and concerns. They preserved what continued to speak to the needs of the ongoing church. Therefore, in differing situations different elements of the tradition were preserved. A Jewish Christian church which, like that represented in Acts, ch. 11, as opposing Peter's baptism and admission of a Gentile family, considered the Christian movement as primarily a regeneration and outgrowth of Judaism with room in it only for Gentiles who by circumcision became Jews would be likely to remember chiefly those elements in Jesus' ministry and teaching which could be accommodated to their attitude. The very bulwark of their intransigence would be the saying of Jesus that he was "not sent but unto the lost sheep of the house of Israel" and his practice in his ministry of limiting the scope of his mission to his own people. But those who very early, like Paul, recognized in the gospel an offer of life that was destined for all mankind had sensitive ears for everything in the traditions that pointed beyond Israel to the Gentiles and they may well have sharpened such elements in order to make them more obvious. That the issue between these two interpretations came early to the surface is much more evident in Paul's letters than in the book of Acts. Paul, as the most aggressive proponent of the mission to the Gentiles, suffered severely at the hands of those who wished to preserve the distinctively Jewish character of the church. How powerful his opponents were in the Jerusalem church is made clear in Gal., ch. 2, where messengers representing James, the brother of Jesus and the head of the Jerusalem church, protested at Antioch against Christian Jews disobeying the kosher food laws by eating at the same table with Christian Gentiles and persuaded even Peter to compromise the universality of the gospel. The attempt is made frequently to attribute this Jewish exclusiveness to only a small and troublesome element in the Jewish Christian church in Jerusalem, an attempt that receives some limited support from Acts, but this minimizes the dimensions of the problem and is in direct contradiction to what Paul tells us in Gal., ch. 2, concerning the situation. Galatians is the primary document, by far the closest to the problem historically, while Acts is a late first-century product for which these early contentions have faded into the distance and are no longer important in a unified church. It is surely significant that in Acts, in spite of the precedence given to Peter's conversion of the family of Cornelius, there is no suggestion that either Peter or any others of the Twelve launched out on missions to the Gentiles. This corresponds exactly with Paul's description in Gal. 2:7 of what actually happened: that Peter, the most progressive of the Twelve, was entrusted with the mission to Jews of the Dispersion while Paul was assigned the mission to Gentiles.

We have, then, to face frankly the disturbing fact that Jesus' original disciples considered their mission as limited only to Jews. Admission of Gentiles constituted exceptions to a general rule. Insofar as their mission had universality, it was a mission to Jews scattered throughout the whole world. But, before we criticize them too severely for this limited outlook, we must recognize how definite a limitation Jesus set upon his own mission. Any suggestion that the words "I am not sent but unto the lost sheep of the house of Israel" were put in Jesus' mouth by a narrowly Judaizing church is contradicted by the absence of any record of a mission of Jesus to Gentiles. Contacts with Gentiles during his ministry are rare exceptions. Yet Jesus was in the neighborhood of Gentiles throughout his life. The Decapolis consisted of ten city-states on the pattern of the Greek city-state and with all the elements, cultural, political and religious, of a Greek city. Jerash in Transjordania had two theaters for the presentation of Greek drama. Another row of Greek cities ranged up the Palestinian coast. Gentiles and Gentile life were to be found all through Palestine. Yet Jesus undertook no mission to Gentiles. Like the prophets before him, and like Paul afterward, he had a commission from God that specifically defined his "sending." The primary focus of his ministry was not

upon the Jews of the synagogue or the Gentiles of Palestine but
upon those who belonged by birth to Israel but for one reason
or another had lost their participation in the heritage and destiny
of Israel. We are so conscious of the universality of Jesus' gospel
and of his significance for the whole world that we find it difficult
to grasp the reality of this limitation upon his earthly ministry
and to understand that it in no way contradicts an intrinsic universal intention of that ministry and gospel. But once we grasp
it, and along with it the extent to which Jesus lived his whole life
as a faithful member of the Jewish religious community—critical,
nonconformist, yet faithful—we begin to understand how his
own most intimate disciples could think that their commission
too was limited to the endeavor to restore a scattered and blinded
Israel to its true destiny as the people of God. They, too, were
not sent but unto the lost sheep of the house of Israel (Matt.
10:5). Jesus himself had specifically forbidden them to approach
the Gentiles or the Samaritans.

This limitation of scope in Jesus' definition of his own and his
disciples' mission has to be seen against the background of the
Old Testament. Universality and particularity, which seem at
first to contradict each other, are there held constantly in balance
with each other, with particularity often threatening to over-
balance the universality. God's call to Abraham to be the father
of a particular people belongs in the setting of God's purpose for
his whole creation and all mankind. The singling out of one
people is that through them all men and nations may ultimately
be restored to their true life as God's creatures. The covenant
with Israel exists not just for the sake of Israel but as the first
fruits of a life that must ultimately become the life of all men.
The great prophets never lost this perspective however blind
their people became to it. In The Book of Jonah one of them
ridiculed his countrymen for thinking they could stand in the
succession of the prophets and yet refuse their mission as servant
of a redemption that would embrace the Gentiles. Second Isaiah
comprehended all mankind in the gracious purpose of God; he
heard God saying: "From my mouth has gone forth a word in
righteousness that shall not return: 'To me every knee shall bow,

every tongue shall swear'" (Isa. 45:23). But Second Isaiah provides the most specific background for our problem when he sees two stages in God's work of redemption, first the restoration of Israel to its true purpose and destiny as the servant people of God, and then the shining forth from a restored Israel of a light to lighten the world (Isa. 49:5–6).

It is not possible for one moment to think of Jesus as less universal in his vision than Genesis, or Jeremiah, or Second Isaiah, or The Book of Jonah. He and his gospel carry the Old Testament to its ultimate fulfillment. But for him as for Second Isaiah the universality of the vision did not result in any diminishing of the importance of God's servant people. The universal goal could be reached only by way of a restoration of the servant nation. Upon that restoration Jesus concentrated both his own mission and that of his first disciples, but that was only preparatory to the larger fruition when Israel restored would be the light of the world. The one danger was that the temporary limitation of scope would be misunderstood and would be perverted by Jewish national sentiment into a permanent restriction upon the outreach of the gospel. The factors that entered into the limitation can only be surmised: the priority of the Jews in the order of God's working (similar to Paul's "the Jew first, then the Greek"), their centuries of preparation for his gospel, his love for his own people, the shortness of the time which called for a concentration of his energies, perhaps also an inability to speak the language of the Gentiles. But one factor which was not present was any narrowing of the scope of the care and concern of God for man. There cannot be detected in Jesus any element of Jewish exclusiveness toward Gentile or Samaritan. His ecstatic joy when on a few exceptional occasions Gentiles responded to him with faith is proof of the one and the place accorded a Samaritan in one of his parables is proof of the other.

We have now to take one final step in establishing the setting of our story. The Twelve, we have observed, were characterized in the early church by an attitude of Jewish exclusiveness so far as their own ministry was concerned. They were not unwilling that the gospel should be preached by others to Samaritans and

Gentiles and they gave Paul the right hand of fellowship to affirm their essential unity with him. They are thus to be distinguished from the Judaizers who fought Paul and insisted that Gentiles to be Christians must be circumcised. But they shared with their fellow Jews an intense loyalty to Jewish institutions, were insistent that Christian Jews should combine faithfulness in basic Jewish practices with their Christian faith, and discharged their own apostleship usually within an exclusively Jewish world. It is clear that their sincere devotion to the gospel was being combined with an equally sincere devotion to their national religious and cultural heritage. But if this was true of them in the period after Jesus' death and resurrection, we can surmise that it was equally true of them before Jesus' death. And it would be inevitable that a nationalism of this kind, with its blind spot where Gentiles were concerned, should lead to a misinterpretation of the limitation placed on their mission. In the religious code of Judaism, Gentiles were classified as sinners and as such had no claim upon the compassion of a godly man. Jesus' ignoring of the Gentile world sounded dangerously like this.

Here, then, is a possible setting for our story as Matthew tells it. If Jesus found his disciples harboring such nationalistic prejudice against Gentiles and thereby misunderstanding the limit he had set to their mission, is it conceivable that he would do nothing to set them right? And what more likely occasion could he find for his critique than an encounter with a Gentile woman who was desperately concerned for her demon-possessed daughter and somehow passionately confident in the power of Jesus to help her?

THE STORY IN ITS PROPER SETTING

The silence of Jesus when the Canaanite woman first made her plea for help has usually been interpreted only in relation to her. But when we recognize that in the story Jesus is using his two-edged sword and cutting in two directions at once, the silence takes on a very different significance. The delay in answering the woman had the disciples in view. The idea that Jesus hesitated because he was uncertain whether or not he should respond to the need of a Gentile is ridiculous, particularly in the light of his eventual praise of the woman's faith. It was a strategic hesitation, utilizing the encounter with a Gentile to draw out and expose the discriminatory prejudice of the disciples. Their response was immediate: "Send her away, for she is crying after us." Many commentators interpret this to mean, "Send her away with her request granted." Understanding Jesus' silence as an unwillingness to help the woman, they make the disciples plead her case and take Jesus' answer in v. 24 as addressed to the disciples, explaining to them why he cannot respond to a Gentile woman. But this ignores the obvious meaning of the disciples' words in v. 23. They want to get rid of the woman. Her importunity is an annoyance to them. They would not have responded in that way if the woman had been Jewish. Her need and her expectation would have won them to her side. It was her foreign nationality that set them against her and made them insensitive to her plight.

Jesus' first words, in v. 24, then, were spoken to the woman, apparently in compliance with the demand of his disciples. They are the words which the disciples, then and later, used as the validation of their attitude toward Gentiles. Jesus was playing a part. There is a parallel here with Jesus' handling of the lawyer in the dialogue which led up to the parable of the good Samaritan. There he led the lawyer on to make a fool of himself before the crowd. Here he leads his disciples on to expose their prejudice against Gentiles. He was playing a deadly serious game with them. But at the same time he was playing a game necessarily also with the woman, and it was essential to his purpose that she should understand, however rudely forbidding his words should sound on the surface, that he was definitely not sending her away. We have here, perhaps, an instance of how a person may say one thing with his words and something quite different with his eyes. Certainly the woman did not interpret Jesus' silence or his statement that his mission was limited to Israel as making it useless for her to persist. Her brief response, "Lord, help me," which should perhaps be translated, "Sir, help me," reflects confidence and impatience rather than despair. In a moment we shall find her, to Jesus' delight, entering into the spirit of his game, but at this stage she seems only to be puzzled by the conversation. Luther, in his comment on the passage, rightly saw that the woman heard a "yes" in Jesus' "no."

It is Jesus' second statement, in v. 26, that has embarrassed and perplexed Christians for centuries. It is so narrow-hearted and cruel that it is completely incongruous in the mouth of Jesus. "It is not fair to take the children's bread and cast it to dogs." Are Jews alone the children of God? Is the bread of God's healing grace intended only for Jews? Are Gentiles to be considered no better than dogs? The attempts to find ways of softening the harshness of the words are futile. The dogs are not pet dogs. For a Hebrew to call anyone a dog was to express his scorn and disparagement. Jesus intended the words to be harsh and cruel because they had to expose the full harshness and heartlessness of nationalistic prejudice against foreigners. Had they been spoken by Jesus to the woman as a sincere expression of his own mind, they would not only have crushed her and sent her fleeing but they would have spelled the end of his ministry to mankind. But she is not crushed at all. Far from it! She shows a complete assurance that Jesus is not against her but for her. He and she understand each other. His words convey to her something completely different from what they seem to say. She seizes upon his harshest word "dogs" and embraces it. She will gladly be his dog if he will be her master and let some of the crumbs from his table fall to her!

The game is over. Not only has the prejudice of the disciples been exposed but also the marvelous faith of the Gentile woman. Jesus had no need to turn and rebuke the disciples. They knew well enough what he had been doing with them, that his words about "children's bread" and "dogs" were expressions not of his own mind and heart but of theirs. And when he exclaimed, "O woman, great is your faith!" he was at one and the same time commending the faith of a woman whom they had wanted to send away and rebuking the narrowness and blindness in them that had steeled them against her.

It is not difficult to identify the context in which this story would be preserved. The early church in Jerusalem as it is portrayed in Acts seems to have a double character, the Aramaic-speaking church of the Twelve showing little interest in breaking out beyond the limits of the Jewish community (even Peter required a special revelation to make him willing to approach Gentiles), but the Greek-speaking church of Stephen and Philip being much more adventurous and open to the greater world beyond. The former emphasized the Jewishness of Jesus, his conformity in the main with the patterns of Jewish life, the focus of his ministry on Jews, and the necessity for Jewish Christians to model their conduct on his, but to the latter the ministry and gospel of Jesus were more radical, his directing of his mission to the lost sheep of the house of Israel being just the first step toward the redemption of a lost world. It would be among these Hellenist Christians that the encounter of Jesus with the Canaanite woman would be remembered and it would be an important element in the validation of their missionary enterprise in the face of criticism from the more conservative wing of the church. Only when the original context and the original meaning of the encounter had been forgotten would the seeming harshness of Jesus' words become an embarrassment and result in the reduction of the form of the story to what has been preserved in Mark.

SOME FINAL NOTES

Anyone who is shocked that Jesus' disciples should have placed a woman beyond the bounds of their compassion merely because she was a foreigner is most likely blind to the power of nationalism in our own time. Racial and national prejudices operate just as effectively and in much the same way today as they did then and they are as inexcusable with American, British, French, or German Christians as they are with first-century Jewish Christians. It is striking and astounding how among what seem to be devoted Christians the wrong skin color or the wrong racial origin can dry up the wells of compassion. People who are horrified at a brutal murder in their own city can condone the bombing of thousands of women and children in their homes in a foreign country across the ocean. We ought not to be surprised that the first disciples let their devotion to Jesus' gospel become intermingled and compromised by fusion with their devotion to their Jewish nation and culture. It is what happens constantly to the Christian faith and it has undoubtedly happened with us whether we are aware of it or not. In fact, it seems to be our most besetting sin in the modern world that we let the Christian faith become so fused and confused with the values of our various national cultures that it is in danger of being hopelessly compromised and concealed.

Chapter VI

JESUS' ENCOUNTER
WITH A MAN OF WEALTH

WE HAVE OUR CHOICE among three versions of Jesus' encounter with a man of wealth, two closely similar and the third, the Matthean, with significant variations that show it to be distinctly later. The account in Mark 10:17–27 is clearly the earliest and the most vivid. The man of wealth is usually called the rich young ruler, but for Mark he is neither young nor a member of the Sanhedrin. That he is not young is evident in the assertion that he has kept the commandments "from my youth up." It is Matthew who makes him young, omitting the phrase "from my youth up." And it is Luke who makes him a ruler, inferring from his great wealth most likely that he would be a member of the Sanhedrin. But it is Mark who preserves the vivid touches— that this man of wealth knelt to Jesus before asking his question and that Jesus, looking on him, loved him, which suggests that Jesus would gladly have had him as one of the group of disciples who traveled with him, sharing in his mission. It is strange that Luke should omit such details, for he retains and even heightens them in other traditions. It may be that, conceiving the rich man as a distinguished member of the ruling council, he found it inappropriate to represent him kneeling to Jesus or viewed as a prospect for intimate discipleship.

The version in Matt. 19:16–26 is chiefly interesting in that it shows the problems which the Marcan tradition furnished for one section of the early church. In Mark, Jesus' criticism of the man for addressing him as *"Good* Master" and his assertion that

there is no one good except God seemed to contradict the
church's conception of Jesus as sinless in his divinity. Therefore,
in Matthew the adjective "good" was omitted from the words of
address, and Jesus was made to criticize rather pointlessly and
unreasonably an inquiry concerning goodness. Also, according
to the best manuscripts, the word "God" was omitted from the
next sentence, leaving its meaning vague and ambiguous. For
some reason, Matthew felt it necessary to make the man young
and to give him a larger part in the dialogue. When Jesus tells
him to keep the commandments, he asks, "Which ones?" making Jesus' answer, in which, incidentally, "You shall love your
neighbor as yourself" is added, not a sampling of all the commandments but a detailing of the ones that are essential to gain
eternal life! Again it is the young man who is made to ask, "What
lack I yet?" instead of Matthew's having Jesus discern the lack
and, like a good physician, put his finger on the spot where the
man's relationship with God is broken. Matthew, like Luke, is
unable to see this man of wealth as a prospective disciple and
gives the story a quite different turn by having Jesus say to him,
"If you would be perfect, go sell what you have." The problem
thereby ceases to be one of enlisting the man as a full-time
disciple, sharing a life of poverty with Jesus and the others, and
becomes one of how a good religious man is to reach moral and
spiritual perfection. This modification has in it also, perhaps, a
softening of the application of the command to "sell all." The
command was addressed only to a man who desired to attain
perfection.

We can understand the Matthean church having difficulty
with the earliest form of the story. It is still disturbing to many
Christians to have Jesus refuse to let a man call him good and
forbid the use of the term "good" for anyone except God. But
there are other difficulties. Is Jesus to be understood as saying
to this man in v. 19 that keeping the commandments is sufficient
to earn him eternal life? Why does Jesus select this particular
series of commandments? Then, more seriously, does he really
demand of anyone who would be his disciple the surrender of all
his possessions and a life of poverty? And, most seriously of all,

why would Jesus let such a promising man—humble, deeply religious, with great possibilities for service, powerfully attracted by Jesus and his teaching (for we must assume that he had heard Jesus preaching or teaching and in response was drawn to Jesus even as we see him in the encounter), with financial resources that would have been very useful to the mission—go sadly away? Why did Jesus lose him when any one of Jesus' ministers today would be ashamed of himself if he could not win the man and make him a staunch member of the church? It is a troublesome story. Matthew lets us see how early it was felt to be troublesome, which gives us assurance that the story as Mark tells it is not one that any section of the early church would be likely to have invented. The story was remembered in spite of the discomfort it caused, for it kept alive in the church the consciousness of what a difficult person Jesus had been to live with and how essential the discomfort of his presence and the severity of his approach to men was to the accomplishment of his mission.

THE PROBLEM BEHIND THE WORD "GOOD"

The question of the inquirer with which the scene opens furnishes an excellent illustration of how identical words may have a very different meaning. It is the same question that the legalist asked in the introduction to the parable of the good Samaritan. There it was asked as a test question to see whether Jesus would answer in an orthodox fashion and, if possible, to trip him up. But here it is the earnest inquiry of a man who is profoundly concerned about his soul's good. The last thing the lawyer in the other scene would have thought of doing would have been to kneel to Jesus or to confess any lack in himself. It may have been this superficial parallel between the two scenes that caused Matthew to add, "Thou shalt love thy neighbor as thyself" to the list of commandments. Further, a comparison of Mark 10:17 with v. 23 shows that "eternal life" is understood as a synonym for "Kingdom of God." The man has heard Jesus preaching his gospel of the Kingdom and is aware of it as a life that is still beyond him in spite of his scrupulousness in the keeping of the commandments. He wants to share in the life of the new age that Jesus has been holding before men as God's promise to faith. It was to be nothing less than a transformation of human existence. Jesus had demanded repentance of all who would enter the Kingdom, and this man was ready for repentance if only Jesus would show him where he needed to repent and what he must do that he was not already doing.

Jesus' ignoring of the substance of the man's opening question, seizing upon a single word as symptomatic of the man's spiritual condition, and quickly thrusting at him a question that seemingly had no relation to what he had asked, is sufficiently often a characteristic of Jesus' dialogue with persons to make it a distinct memory of his way of working. It is interesting that in the Gospel of John, in the dialogue with the woman of Samaria in ch. 4, this characteristic is schematized in a mechanical fashion, Jesus invariably answering each question with a question of his own that strikes under the woman's guard at the problem of her soul. It fits with Jesus' conception of himself as a physician whose task it was to diagnose the diseases of men's souls and, laying bare the hidden trouble, bring healing and health. The way in which this man said, "Good Master," revealed to Jesus his whole outlook on religion and life. Godliness was for him essentially a matter of being good, of doing the right thing, of never offending against any of the laws of God or man. If one's life were blameless, then surely God would reward such goodness and obedience with eternal life. The man was not in any doubt about his own goodness. Jesus would draw that admission from him shortly. His only uncertainty was whether he was as yet good enough to merit eternal life. Always in a religion of merit there is a haunting suspicion of inadequacy. The complacency of self-justification is shaken from time to time by an awareness of something wrong at a deeper level, by a weariness and boredom with being good, by a sense of vacancy where according to all the best traditions there should be the joy and confidence and vitality of a creative relation with God. If this man had already been exposed to Jesus' preaching, it is no wonder that he was conscious of something he needed beyond the blamelessness of his past performance. And yet his customary way of thinking came out in his first word. The most respectful term he could use in addressing Jesus was "good." He thought of Jesus as good in a way that was superior to the way in which he himself was good. But the two of them already had this in common, that they were both good. He expected Jesus to initiate him into his superior goodness, to show him what he must do beyond what he was doing, to help him move one stage higher in his progress in goodness. He had no thought of anything beyond a religion of works by which one should be able eventually to inherit eternal life.

Against this background we can understand why Jesus struck so sharply at the man's use of the word "good." Matthew eliminates any discussion of Jesus' goodness by detaching the adjective "good" from "master" and attaching it to the following word in the Greek sentence to read, "What good thing must I do?" This accentuates, however, the moralism of the questioner of which Jesus had good reason to be critical. To Jesus as to Paul it was basic that all men are sinners; all men are sick in their relation with God and with each other; all men are in debt to God in such a way that their only hope of liberation lies in God's forgiveness. We can leave aside for the moment whether or not Jesus was confessing himself a sinner. The point of his penetrating question and blunt assertion that no man should be called good was before all else intended to smash through the complacency of a religion of works that to him was simply a false and blind road on which no man would ever find the living God. The man who can count himself good has simply never stood before God and known God's estimate of him, God's judgment upon him.

Basic to the relation between God and man is God's sovereignty, God's claim to precedence over all the other loyalties, relationships, and interests of man. With good reason the first commandment is "Thou shalt have no other gods beside me." This had warmer expression in the Shema, "Thou shalt love the Lord thy God with all thy heart, and with all thy soul, and with all thy might." Jesus reexpressed it when he said, "Seek ye first the Kingdom of God and his righteousness," and underlying all of Jesus' teaching is the claim of God to an unconditional sovereignty over man's life. Faith is man's unconditional openness to God and where it is present in the slightest degree the power of God that can move mountains is present. The tragic mistake of men is that, jealous of their own self-sovereignty, they concede to God only a conditional sovereignty over their lives. They identify their lives with their own self-rule and see God's radical claim as a threat to their existence. They defend themselves and their world against the threat, and the most effective defense they can find is a religion of merit in which a measure of obedience to God becomes in their eyes a reasonable substitute for the total surrender that God claims. Paul was later to call this "establishing one's own righteousness," which he himself had eventually found to be an exercise in futility.

This, then, was the sterile religion of the established order in which Jesus saw the men of his time imprisoned and against which he was in rebellion. It was his task to liberate them from it, and, confronted with our man of wealth, Jesus knew that he had to shake him loose from his complacency and his confidence in his own goodness before he could be reached. The man's estimate of himself as a good man in a society of essentially good men who needed only to be shown how to improve upon their goodness had to be shattered. Hence Jesus' first words to him: a rebuke for calling him good and a second rebuke for not knowing that in the light of God's goodness no man can be called good. Against this background it is impossible to interpret Mark 10:19 as though Jesus were suggesting that a keeping of the commandments is sufficient for one to gain eternal life. The verse can be rightly understood only when it is seen in the context of what comes before and after, as the transition between Jesus' first attack on the man's problem and his second attack in which he put his finger directly on the point of failure and proposed a drastic remedy. Jesus, by his reference to the commandments, led the man to show himself simply as he was. He was not conscious of any commandment that he had broken from the time he was a child. Jesus apparently saw two things in that confession. He recognized a passionate zeal for God and a desire to be right before God that now had made the man respond to what he heard in Jesus' preaching, and "looking on him, Jesus loved him" and wanted him for a disciple. But he saw also the imprisonment of the man in his religion of works and the futility of his zeal for God because in himself he was really not yet free for God. He no doubt considered himself to be a man who loved God with all his heart and soul and put God first at all times, but the reality, recognized by Jesus, was that his wealth came first and God came second. If there had to be a choice between his God and his great possessions, with all the comfort, prestige, and power that they provided for him, he would find himself sadly torn but he would choose the latter. And in that choice it would be evident that his possessions were more essential to him than his God.

Jesus set him before the choice. Here again we see the ruthlessness of Jesus when a man's whole destiny was in the balance. It was all or nothing. What did he see in this man? Another Peter, an apostle who would carry the gospel over sea and land? There was a destiny waiting for him if only he could be captured. But he had to be truly captured, committed with no conditions or qualifications. He had to be free for God and for whatever God would ask of him. There can be no question but that Jesus intended him to be one of those closest to him, actively engaged in the extension of his mission. One of the conditions of participation from the beginning had been the abandonment of any concern about possessions or support. Jesus himself had nothing he could call his own, and the disciples had left everything to share his mission. They were dependent on what was given them to supply their needs each day. But surely it was unreasonable to think that a man of great wealth would suddenly give it all away in order to share the mission and the poverty of Jesus! By "reasonable" we mean "what can be normally expected," and we forget that Jesus was the spearhead of a revolutionary invasion of the established order by the new age of the Kingdom. He calculated not on what can normally be expected but on what can happen when men's lives are laid open to the presence and power of God. The man before him was on the verge of faith. He had responded to the gospel of the Kingdom and was reaching out for a life in God that would carry him beyond anything he had as yet known. But Jesus had no strategy with which to ease him into the Kingdom, no subtle compromise with which to dissolve the necessity for a decision between God and possessions. So the man of promise was allowed to go sadly away. We tell ourselves that Jesus was too ruthless, too demanding. *We* could have solved the problem without compromising the conditions of faith and so have gained the man and his resources for the cause. We do it all the time. But judging by the quality of discipleship that results from each of the approaches, his and ours, are we sure that from the standpoint of God's interest and God's cause our approach is the most reasonable and the most practical?

POSSESSIONS AS AN OBSTACLE TO FAITH

We still have two thorny problems on our hands as a consequence of this tradition. The first, which is particularly thorny in a church most of whose members are comfortably provided with possessions, is whether or not Jesus made poverty a necessary condition of true discipleship. The story was so interpreted in the second century of the church's life and became the charter of the monastic orders that were dedicated to lives of poverty, holding that they alone were going the whole way with Jesus, sharing with him his poverty in order to possess no riches but those of the Kingdom of God. But the poverty of monks and hermits frequently took on an unworldly character quite different from that of the poverty of Jesus and the disciples. For Jesus and the early church, poverty was not an aspect of flight from an evil world but, rather, an aspect of their freedom to be completely at God's service for the invasion of the world with God's new age.

We have already seen that Jesus' demand to "sell all and give to the poor" was not a laying down of a general condition of faith but has to be understood in the context of his dealing with this one man's situation. There is no evidence that Jesus made a similar demand on all who responded to him. To be a member of the intimate group that traveled with him was to accept poverty as a condition of life, and most certainly to be a son of the Kingdom was to sit loose to all possessions. But Christians quite clearly did not at once free themselves of everything they owned. Zacchaeus, in Luke, ch. 19, gives only half of his wealth to the poor. The mother of Mark still owned a house large enough for the early Christians to meet in.

But we must guard ourselves against dissolving the severity of Jesus' words concerning possessions. In Jesus' conversation with his disciples after the departure of the man of wealth, Mark represents Jesus as saying twice over how hard it is for those who have riches and trust in them to enter the Kingdom of God, to which then is added the analogy of the camel seeking to go through the eye of a needle. Some ingenious apologists have devised the story that there was a gate in a wall called "the needle's eye" which a camel could enter only by going down on its knees, so that Jesus' meaning was only that rich men have to be humbled to enter the Kingdom. Such an explanation is not only devious but misses entirely the point of the vivid phrase. It is an Oriental exaggeration to express the difficulty of what was being attempted, like the parallel image of the man who "strains at a gnat and swallows a camel." The disciples clearly understood Jesus to be saying that it was impossible for a rich man to enter the Kingdom. In Mark 10:27, Jesus had to condition his own statement by assuring them that, though it was humanly impossible, it was still possible by God's grace. But it is impossible to evade the fact that Jesus regarded possessions as a serious obstacle to the kind of faith in which a man is unconditionally at God's disposal. Family relationships and possessions were, and are, God's closest competitors for first place in human affection. Then as now it was generally taken for granted that these should be first, and then as now it was felt to be offensive and unreasonable for Jesus to claim for the Kingdom a precedence over both. Yet it was this radical claim for God that accounted for one of the most distinctive and impressive features of the early church, the willingness of its members to surrender their private possessions to a common fund that was used to meet the needs of poorer members.

But we must not miss another side to this attitude of Jesus concerning possessions. He had observed that one of the most frequent sources of crippling anxiety in life was concern about food, clothing, and housing. It was not necessary to have great possessions, in fact it was not necessary to have any possessions, in order to have one's whole being consumed by care about them. It was not just among the wealthy but also among the poor, with whom Jesus was much more familiar, that God was relegated to second place by pressing material concerns. Therefore, one aspect of Jesus' mission was to free men from this all-consuming anxiety. Life can have its true and healthy order only when the Kingdom and its concerns are first and the material needs are kept firmly in a subordinate place. It would seem to be closer to Jesus' mind to speak of possessions rather than of riches. The word "rich" is a very relative term that gives men opportunity to evade the force of Jesus' claim. To those millions of workmen in the world who earn less than a dollar a day, a wage of ten dollars a day is wealth, but ten dollars a day on the North American continent is counted poverty. The problem may become more acute with the increase of possessions but it is present wherever there are possessions. Even at the most minimal level they challenge the precedence of God in a man's life. The question is, Where do we seek our security and our ultimate satisfaction, and what is the basis of our confidence and trust?

The Sinlessness of Jesus

There is still the question that bothered the author of Matthew's Gospel, whether Jesus in this encounter confessed himself a sinner like all other men. Certainly in the original story he refused to let himself be called good and supported his refusal with the assertion that in the light of God's goodness no human being should be called good. Luke found nothing objectionable in this, but Matthew did. For Matthew, it contradicted the church's doctrine of the sinlessness of Jesus which was a corollary of his divinity.

This concept of sinlessness is in need of examination because, understood in one familiar sense, it can make of Jesus a static divine figure who could have no human historical existence, a Jesus who could not make a mistake even in his first attempts at writing or arithmetic, a Jesus who did not have to learn anything, since he knew it all already. Luke dismissed this docetic Jesus when he described the boy Jesus as growing in wisdom as well as stature and in favor with God and man.

The traditional Roman Catholic concept of sinlessness, like the Jewish one of blamelessness, rests upon a deficient understanding of sin. Paul could think of himself as blameless as long as sin was defined as disobedience to any of the prescribed laws, but when it was unveiled to him by the cross as a resistance of the human self to God, which could clothe itself defensively in all the garments of morality and religion, he was forever undone and without excuse before God. So also Luther knew that the Christian saint never ceases to be a sinner to his dying day. The resistance of the self to God is of such a tenacity that it is never completely overcome in a lifetime. Therefore, sinlessness of the Roman Catholic or Jewish kind belongs in an essentially non-Christian or legalistic context. The sinlessness of Jesus Christ, however, has to be understood in the distinctively Christian context where it is an assertion not of some kind of inerrancy but of the oneness of his human will with the will of the Father, a oneness that was not static but dynamic, preserved at an infinite cost by his constantly renewed obedience to God. We should, perhaps, speak of the perfect obedience of Christ rather than of his sinlessness. The mystery and miracle of Jesus is his oneness with God in personal relation, in which his person is not dissolved into a static divinity but resolved into the most dynamic fulfillment of a human existence. He is man in the fullest measure, one of us, so identified with us in our blind and broken human selves that he felt the burden of our sin as though it were his own, and yet in him we can find no brokenness or shadow in his relation with the Father. Thus, in the encounter that we have been considering, it is unthinkable that he should have made an exception for himself. In fact, it is unthinkable that Jesus should ever have spoken of his own sinlessness or of his perfect obedience to God. What is fitting and necessary for his church to say of him was neither fitting nor necessary for him to say of himself.

Chapter VII

JESUS AND JUDAS

THE DEATH OF JESUS is not usually considered an assassination, and yet it was, and Judas was the assassin. He murdered Jesus as definitely as though he had plunged a knife into his heart. He betrayed Jesus into the hands of men who feared and hated him and were certain to send him to his death. We always find it difficult to understand why anyone would hate or fear Jesus sufficiently to desire his death, and especially why religious and political leaders would bypass the ordinary processes of justice in their eagerness for his death. He had injured no man. The one purpose for which he lived was to help his fellowmen at the two points where they most needed help, in their relations with God and with each other. He was the friend of the poor, of the sick in body and mind, and of the outcast. He proclaimed the dawn of a new age in which love instead of fear and hatred and greed would rule the lives of men, and he went about enlisting men as citizens of that new age, but he forced his teachings and convictions on no one. Compulsion was completely alien to his spirit. Why, then, would men want him dead? The answer remains a mystery until we grasp how revolutionary Jesus' seemingly so peaceful and spiritual teaching was. His new age was already changing men's lives, creating new attitudes to everything in life, and if it kept moving in on the community, the whole established order of religion and society would be endangered. It meant change and change was what many people were determined should not take place. The assassination of

Martin Luther King has shown us how people who count themselves not only responsible citizens but Christians can be glad
for the death of a man who threatened their society with radical
change.

But what makes the death of Jesus a much deeper mystery is
that the assassin should have been a committed disciple, a member of the group of twelve who had given up everything to share
his mission and had been trained by him to preach, teach, and
heal even as he himself was doing. A Lee Harvey Oswald, when
he shoots down President John F. Kennedy, is consciously or
unconsciously fulfilling the desire of a host of conservative enemies of Kennedy who have made no secret of their hatred of him.
The murderer of Martin Luther King, whatever his motive, did
what thousands who feared and hated King wanted done in order
to put an end to the program of Negro emancipation. The Jor-
danian assassin of Robert Kennedy saw himself as the representative of the Arab community that had been dispossessed by the
Israelis, and Robert Kennedy as a further threat to his people's
welfare. But Judas was the intimate friend and follower of his
victim. He had been chosen as one of the Twelve because of his
response to the gospel and his commitment to the new age. He
had been constantly in Jesus' company for months. He had eaten
his meals with Jesus, traveled with him, listened to him, talked
with him, slept with him; and then suddenly he turned against
him and sent him to his death. Why did he do it? How are we to
understand this strange betrayal and, we must say, assassination
of Jesus?

A whole series of explanations have been offered, some more
interesting than others but none of them adequate. There is one
that begins by asserting that Jesus' death was necessary for the
redemption of mankind and that Judas was placed in the disciple
group by God, with Jesus' cooperation of course, for the express
purpose of securing Jesus' sacrificial death. It was all arranged
by God. It is curious that anyone familiar with Scripture could
invent such a scheme in which men are reduced to puppets and
events take place when God manipulates the strings. There are
no puppets in the Bible, but only men acting in freedom and

responsibility. Judas was a man of flesh and blood with human motives for what he did. What God made of his deed when it was done is another matter. Moreover, it was quite unnecessary for God to hide a traitor in the disciple group in order to secure Jesus' death. Had Judas not acted, the authorities would undoubtedly have found some other means to put an end to Jesus' mission.

An explanation that has been put forward in different quarters, with variations, and that many seem to find attractive, attempts to maintain Judas' integrity as a disciple. Where he went wrong was in his overeagerness for the coming of the new age. He wanted to see the present evil order swept away and the Kingdom of God established in the land with power. He had no doubt that Jesus was God's Messianic King and he could not understand why Jesus did not bring the present preliminary stage of preaching, teaching, and healing to an end and begin his Messianic rule. Jesus was too hesitant for him. Therefore, he meant only to force Jesus' hand when he roused the authorities against him, being quite certain that in the ensuing struggle the Messiah could not go down to defeat but with God's help would establish his Kingdom, in which each of the disciples would have a place of high responsibility. When he saw that his strategy had failed, he hanged himself in despair. The theory is pure conjecture with no support in the records. The assumption of all the traditions is that the act was one of stark betrayal and that Judas let himself be used as an agent of the evil forces that were pitted against Jesus.

A third interpretation that receives more support from the Gospels makes of Judas an incarnation of Satan. Luke 22:3 says, "Satan entered into Judas." John 13:2 says that the devil put it in Judas' heart to betray Jesus and ch. 17:12 has Jesus call him "the son of perdition." The danger here is that Judas should be made a puppet of Satan, no longer driven by ordinary or extraordinary human motives, and should thereby be removed from our familiar world. But that is not the intention of those responsible for the gospel tradition. When Jesus said to Peter, "Get thee behind me, Satan," he was not reducing Peter to a puppet of

Satan but was merely identifying Peter's well-meant protest against his Master's foreboding of tragedy as nothing less than an attempt of the power that resists God's purpose in the world to deflect him from the course that he saw opening before him. If Jesus could address Peter as Satan, then all the more the church could think of Judas as the very incarnation of Satan without reducing him to a puppet in the control of a supernatural evil power. What must not happen is that Judas should cease to be responsible for what he did. He must remain one of us or he will lose all meaning for us. The passion play at Oberammergau, in representing him as a low cunning rascal and making him look outwardly ridiculous, has this effect of removing him from the world of humanity with which we are familiar, so that there is no possibility of any identification of him with ourselves or with anyone we know. But the same thing happens in the popular mind far beyond Oberammergau, that he becomes a man who is wholly evil, incomprehensibly evil, and has no longer any share in or likeness to our common humanity.

WHAT WE CAN KNOW OF JUDAS

We need to be warned as we begin to sort out the facts concerning Judas and his relation to Jesus that he may break out of that distant alien realm to which we have consigned him and become steadily and distressingly a figure more familiar to us in our world than we ever dreamed was possible.

We begin at the end of the story as it is depicted in Matt. 27:3–5, for it is in the light of the end that all the rest has to be interpreted. But there are three accounts of Judas' end among which we have to choose, two in the New Testament and one in the fragments of Papias. In the first chapter of Acts, Peter, in speaking of the vacancy in the number of the Twelve made by the death of Judas, is represented as describing Judas' death in this way: having purchased a field, he went there, and swelling up in an enormous fashion, he burst open and his bowels and blood were strewn across the field. Papias has the same tradition of his swelling up but has him die by being caught between the

corner of a house and a passing wagon. Matthew's account is less
spectacular and gory but much more vividly human: when he
saw that Jesus was condemned, he repented of what he had done
and, before the crucifixion, went to the authorities, telling them
that he had betrayed an innocent man, trying to give back the
money he had taken and to persuade them to release Jesus.
When he failed, he threw down the money in the Temple and,
unable to face life with such guilt upon his soul, went and hanged
himself, so that he was dead before ever Jesus went to his cross.
It is not difficult to choose between these three accounts. Two of
them have on them the marks of legend. In the popular mind
suicide by hanging was too easy a death for such a man as Judas.
Some fantastic fate had to be provided for him. We find a
parallel in Acts in the death of the king who for his blasphemy
was consumed by worms as he sat upon his throne. The account
in Matthew, however, is credible in every detail—the repentance
when Jesus was actually condemned to death, the attempt to buy
back his life, and the despair moving swiftly to suicide. However
we picture Judas, he must be a man for whom this could be the
final act in his drama of life. This clearly was no ordinary assassin and no ordinary drama.

Judas' presence among the Twelve who were chosen by Jesus
to share the work of his mission provides us with our first solid
information about him. He was there because Jesus recognized
in him one of those whose response to his gospel was most encouraging for the future. First, Judas somewhere heard Jesus'
proclamation of the coming of the new age and committed himself to it in repentance and faith. He was no mere hanger-on.
What had given his own life new meaning he was willing and
eager to share with others, and when Jesus chose him from
among all his followers to be one of those who would be constantly with him, Judas left his home and his normal occupation
to accept a life of poverty in the group that traveled everywhere
with Jesus. Jesus' choice of him is an indication of the poten-
tiality that he saw in him. Also, he was given the same training as
the others, and when they were sent out in twos to carry on in-
dependently a mission like that of Jesus—preaching, teaching,

healing, and exorcising demons—Judas was a participant. He preached, he taught, he healed, he liberated people from their demon enslavement. We do not begin to draw the portrait of Judas rightly until we grasp that he was an active missionary of Jesus' gospel. This puts an end to all those representations which make him an evil villain who in some incomprehensible way got into the disciple group.

We know also that he was made treasurer of the group. Someone had to take care of whatever money they were given to provide for their daily necessities, and Judas was appointed. This surely was a mark of the group's confidence in him and suggests also that he was recognized as the one best fitted to take care of such matters. An organization does not commit its funds to a person in whom it has no trust. The Gospel of John preserves an accusation against Judas that he pilfered from the common purse. It is possible to make too much of this. After all, how much was in the purse? Certainly no great amount. A thief would not have had much if he had taken it all. Judas did the spending for the group and apparently he sometimes spent a little on himself. But if he did so and was observed, he would be told of it either by Jesus or by some of his fellow disciples. There is a possibility here of hurt pride and of Judas' feeling personal offense against his companions.

That he was Judas "Iscariot" identifies Judas as a "man of Kerioth." Kerioth has not been definitely located but is thought to have been a town in Judea, which would make Judas the one disciple who came from Judea. All the others were from Galilee. Judeans were notoriously proud of their ancient lineage and regarded themselves as a purer stock, superior to the Galileans, whose population through the centuries had become mixed with aliens. Like all racial pride, the Judean pride was without any basis, for the population of Judea had experienced its own varied mixtures in the forgotten past, but their pride was sufficient to make Judeans say, "Can anything good come out of Nazareth?" We cannot say with certainty that this had any bearing upon the problem of Judas but at least it is there in the background and creates the possibility of a degree of tension between the one Judean and the twelve Galileans.

THE MOTIVE OF THE BETRAYAL

With any such deed as that of Judas it is highly important to locate the motive. The most obvious suggestion is greed—based on the fact that he received thirty pieces of silver from the authorities for what he did. But thirty pieces of silver is a paltry sum, the price of a slave in the market, and not at all an amount with which any man might enrich himself. What about all the income Judas had given up in order to become a member of the mission? A greedy man would hardly have made such a sacrifice, and a sane man would hardly have thought to recoup his loss by selling his prophetic leader to the authorities. Greed is no explanation of the deed. Above all, it is inconceivable that Jesus would have chosen as one of the Twelve a man so blindly in the control of greed. And would a greedy man, when his deed was done, have thrown the money back at his employers and hanged himself?

Another suggestion[27] has been that the motive was jealousy, mixed to some degree with greed. Judas is represented as ambitious for leadership. It grieved him that Peter, James, and John were given such precedence by Jesus. He considered himself much more competent than they. The slight to his pride grew upon him until he could endure it no longer. But surely rivalry for precedence within the group is no adequate motivation for such a desperate act.

It is strange that no one in the discussion of Judas seems ever to have exploited the rather obvious parallel between the pre-Christian Paul and Judas. When Paul attacked the Christians, imprisoning them and attempting to suppress their movement, he did not consider himself to be doing something evil. On the contrary, he was defending the established order of religion in the Israel of God against a subversive teaching that threatened the very foundations of Judaism, and thereby he was serving

God. We sometimes forget what an impressive religious and moral order was constituted by the Judaism of Jesus' day. It claimed a proud superiority over all that was known elsewhere in the world. The Jewish worship, the Jewish faith in God, and the Jewish way of life were purer and nobler by far than those of the Greeks, Romans, Syrians, Egyptians, and Persians. And was not the word of the rabbis to be believed, that the whole order of Judaism was based on the infallible words of God which were preserved intact in every jot and tittle of the sacred Scriptures? Who dared lay hand on such a sacred structure or suggest that it needed to be replaced by some yet more perfect work of God, at least not before the great day when God himself would bring this world to an end and inaugurate his final Kingdom? Paul's fanatical hatred of the Christian movement had behind it this absolutizing of the present religious and social order and a discernment that what Jesus and his followers were saying and doing set all such absolutes in question. A static religion was being threatened by a dynamic faith.

A Jewish rabbi, Jacob Golub, has provided us with the next clue to the solution of our mystery in his interpretation of Judas in a book that he wrote for Jewish high school students, *In the Days of the Second Temple*.[28] He tells the story of the Jewish people from the sixth century B.C. all the way down through and beyond the origin of the Christian movement. He describes the mission and teaching of Jesus, the development of the disciple group, and finally the death of Jesus. But he sees the whole development from the standpoint of one who belongs in continuity with the religious and social structure of Judaism, which was threatened by Jesus, and to Golub, Judas was not a traitor but a patriot. Judas was the one person in the intimate circle about Jesus who ceased to be hypnotized by the new teaching and as a faithful member of the Jewish community recognized how dangerously revolutionary this movement was. If it went on and gained force with the years, it would mean the end of Judaism as it was then established. Nothing eventually would remain the same. The finality of the Jewish Scriptures as the complete and infallible codification of the word of God was being set in question. Jesus seemed to set his own word even above and beyond the sacred Torah. He denied the validity of traditional laws which in Judaism were regarded as laws which were as sacred as any in the Torah. He ridiculed people who thought that by careful obedience to all the prescribed laws they could assure themselves of the favor of God. Where would all this end except in the liquidation of Judaism? But there was one disciple who remained loyal to the faith of his fathers. Judas saw the danger and counted it his duty to turn state's evidence against Jesus. It was comparable to a United States citizen's discovering that a religious leader was actually forwarding a movement which would eventually overthrow the Government. In loyalty to his nation he might well give information to the FBI. Judas would not necessarily anticipate that Jesus would be executed but only that he would be silenced.

It becomes apparent now how much Judas and Paul the Pharisee may have had in common. *Both* of them saw, as others did not, the dangerous implications of Jesus' teachings and influence. It was not obvious on the surface then, just as it is not obvious now. Most Christians today are not aware of anything dangerous or revolutionary in the gospel. Its dynamite is hidden. But suddenly Judas caught sight of it and was frightened by what he saw. The new age to which he had committed himself under the spell of Jesus' words and person would eventually mean the death and disappearance of all that belonged to the old age. Judas would thus seem to have been a man like Paul who saw things more clearly than other men. The insight was to make Paul a leader in the persecution of Christians and then, when he was won over from his loyalty to the old order to a commitment to the new age, it made him the clear-sighted apostle to the Gentiles; both as a Jew and as a Christian, Paul was seized by the revolutionary character of the gospel as few even of the original disciples were. But the same insight made Judas the betrayer of his Master and a despairing suicide.

We have now a much more human picture of Judas and a more adequate explanation of his motive. How strong the loyalty of all the disciples was to Judaism is evident in The Acts of the

Apostles where they are pictured as finding it unthinkable at first
that anyone should be a Christian without at the same time fulfilling the minimal requirements of Judaism. There is a mixture
of nationalism and religious conservatism in this, and it was
present in the Christian community in Jerusalem in various de-
grees of intensity. There were some Jewish Christians who considered Paul the apostle a traitor to his Jewish origins and a per-
verter of Christianity as he broke free from both his nationalism
and his conservatism. It is not difficult therefore to see in Judas,
the proud Judean, one in whom this nationalism and conservatism would be especially strong. Both are passions so deeply
rooted that they can put all reason out of operation, at least for
a moment and sometimes for years, when they are offended.
Religious conservatism that absolutizes some one religious order
and regards any divergence from it or questioning of it as an
attack on God himself has through the centuries sent thousands
of men and women to their deaths and has made life intolerable
for millions. Nationalism is an idolatry equally blinding and even
more destructive. Men are able to commit the most horrible bru-
talities without a twinge of conscience when they are persuaded
that it is necessary for the survival of their nation, or even merely
for the protection of the economic interests of their nation.

The riddle that remains, if Judas acted as a patriot, is why he
was unable to sustain the patriotic and religious justification of
his act for more than twenty-four hours. It was an act of passion,
the kind of passion that drives a man blindly to strike down even
a person whom he loves, but which, when it sees its victim pros-
trate, suddenly has eyes again and cannot bear the sight of what
it has done. Anger is the passion which has these characteristics.
It can blank out for the moment all other considerations, conjure
up out of memory sufficient reasons to justify itself, and for the
moment see in a faithful friend a bitter enemy. But when the
moment has passed and the anger is gone, the justification is
gone with it and there is only despair. We can understand an
anger of Judas at Jesus and at his fellow disciples if he, a proud
Judean, was criticized by Galileans for his conduct as treasurer
of the group. Let this anger be combined with a growing disquiet

that the new age to which he had committed himself was actually a serious threat to the whole order of religion and society in Judaism, and we have a sufficient motivation for the act of Judas. To Judas at the moment it was an act not of treachery but of patriotism. But when he saw Jesus condemned and shortly to be taken out and crucified, the anger ceased to blind him, the memory of all that Jesus and his gospel had meant to him returned, and he knew the horror, the unendurable horror of his act.

We still have the mystery of how a man who had responded to the gospel with a faith that made him willing to give up everything in its service could still be so subject to anger and to blind conservatism and nationalism that he would do such a thing. Eduard Thurneysen, in a sermon[29] on Judas many years ago, suggested an answer that seems to penetrate to the depths of Judas' problem—and to the depths of many problems beyond Judas: Judas was a man who never let himself be quite conquered by Jesus. He responded to the gospel, but it was a limited response. There was a fortress within him which, consciously or unconsciously, he retained for his own sovereignty. He counted himself a citizen of the new age but he was still bound more deeply than he knew by the loyalties of the old age. When a decision had to be made between his nation and the God whom he had come to serve in the company of Jesus, his nation was first and his God second.

If this is a true interpretation, then Judas is no longer a stranger to us, the inhabitant of a different world from ours. He is only too familiar to us. He meets us on every side and we meet him in ourselves. Is it really true that one has only to let his national loyalty, his patriotism, take precedence over his obedience to the God he knows in fellowship with Jesus Christ to be a Judas? The story of the German Church in the days of Hitler is a sobering witness to what happens when Christians let their obedience to Christ become secondary to their obedience to the state. But nationalism is just as blinding in other lands, less obvious perhaps because the nations there are less pagan and brutal than Hitler's Naziism. In fact, the more humane the nation in its general standards, the more difficult it is to recognize that there is a decisive issue between loyalty to nation and loyalty to Jesus Christ. And when Christians are so blind as to think that the professed ideal behind the established order of life within their nation is identical with Christianity, the confusion is complete and the situation ripe for the production of Judases en masse. Judas was not a villian or a pervert or an insane man; he was a minister of the gospel who, when he had to choose between the new age that is promised in the gospel and the established religious and social order in which his life was still rooted, chose that the new should die that the old might live on.

Chapter VIII

JESUS AND PETER

EACH OF THE FIGURES that we have seen in encounter with Jesus has a representative character. This does not set in question the existence of the individual who was originally involved in the encounter but shows only that his individuality has been so remembered in the church that he has become representative of much more than himself. John the Baptist in his relation with Jesus thus comes to represent the relation of Old Testament prophecy to the new age inaugurated by Jesus. Levi the tax collector stands for the world of outsiders in Israel who gave such a welcome to Jesus when he made them his care. The Canaanite woman is symbolic of Jesus' confrontation with the Gentile world, so meager in his lifetime and so important to the church in which the Gospels were finally written. Simon the Pharisee, the expert in law, the man of wealth, and Nicodemus —each of them reflects some one aspect of the religious mind of the Jewish community out of which Jesus came and with which he was in controversy. Judas may seem to us to stand alone, and yet we have seen that in the ultimate analysis he stands together with the pre-Christian Paul and with all who were (and are) offended by the revolutionary character of Jesus' mission and gospel.

This shaping of a historical person into a representative figure, with whom later generations can identify themselves and in whose history they can see their own situation and alternatives reflected, was a deep-rooted aspect of the religious memory of

Israel. The traditions concerning Abraham are an excellent example. He and his trek from Mesopotamia may well be historical, but we do not understand the stories of Abraham's call, his temptations to unfaithfulness, and his many trials of faith until we see that the whole destiny of Israel is incorporated in him and that each new generation saw its life reflected in him as in a mirror. But this did not cease with Israel. In the New Testament, both for Paul and for the author of Hebrews, Abraham in his pilgrimage of faith has come to represent the Christian church. Abraham, going out from his homeland, not knowing for certain his destination but seeking the city that has foundations whose maker and builder is God, is in Hebrews the author's reinterpretation of the Abrahamic tradition to make it representative of the church's inner necessity to move constantly out into new and unexplored regions on its way toward its final goal.

One might expect less of this representative element in the stories of Peter, since he was such a central figure not only in Jesus' lifetime but also in the early church. Surely with him there would be only memories of the man himself. But the opposite is true. Nowhere is the representative quality more evident. He is the representative disciple in the Gospels and in the early chapters of Acts. When Jesus addresses a question to all the disciples as in Matt. 16:13, it is Peter who answers on their behalf. This is frequently misunderstood, the confession of faith in Jesus as the Messiah and the commission of the power of the keys being interpreted as though Peter stood alone, but Matt. 18:18 makes very clear that all the disciples together with Peter received the power of opening and closing the door of the Kingdom (the power of the keys being none other than the power of the word which has this double character: at one and the same time the word of grace and the word of judgment). Only when one searches the Gospels for material about Jesus' relations with members of the Twelve other than Peter and finds how scanty it is for all, and nonexistent for some, does one realize that to a large extent Jesus' relation with Peter was meant in the church's tradition to incorporate Jesus' relation with the Twelve. The same thing is true in the stories of Peter in Acts. The name of

John is placed together with that of Peter in some of the stories, but nothing specific is told of John's words or actions; Peter alone speaks and acts and Peter now is representative of the church. Thus we become aware that the church saw itself in the figure of Peter. Peter's confession, Peter's waywardness, Peter as Satan to Jesus, Peter's denial, Peter's resurrected faith, were remembered not just as incidents in the life of Peter but, as Israel did with Abraham, so the church saw its own fluctuating loyalty reflected in Peter and drew from his story promise for the future. What God did with Peter he could do in each new generation with his church.

Peter's story varies in each of the four Gospels, and from the place he has in each we can deduce something of what place he held in the tradition of the particular church from which that Gospel came. When we examine the evidence, it is clear at once that Peter was most vividly remembered in the Jewish Christian church which lies behind much of the material in Matthew's Gospel. The story of Peter's confession at Caesarea Philippi is much more elaborate in Matthew than in Mark or Luke. There are two passages that occur in Matthew alone, Peter as spokesman for a limited forgiveness in Matt. 18:21–22 and Peter concerned about what reward a disciple should have in Matt. 19:27. Mark is close to Matthew in the amount of attention given to Peter, but Luke has less concerning Peter in his Gospel, and in the Acts he carefully balances the figures of the two leaders, Peter and Paul. In the Gospel of John, Peter no longer holds the central place in the disciple group until ch. 21, which may be a later addition to the original Gospel. Who is intended by "the disciple whom Jesus loved" is debated, and no certain answer can be given, though the disciple John is the most likely identification, but it is certain that in the tradition from which this Gospel comes this other disciple rather than Peter had the central place. The Fourth Gospel has differing versions of Peter's confession and denial and has an additional tradition concerning Peter in the story of the foot washing. At the stage when ch. 21 was added it is clear that Peter has risen out of the subordinate place and is recognized as the chief pastor. This may have been the stage at which the Gospel of John moved out of a narrower stream and was taken up into the broad stream of the church's tradition in which Peter, as we can see from the other Gospels, had had the central place from the beginning.

We are given assurance concerning the essential validity of the church's memory of Peter by the way in which the representation of him in the Gospels corresponds with Paul's depiction of him in the letter to the Galatians. He fluctuates between strength and weakness, between the keenest insight and the grossest blindness, between bold courage and timid compromise. Matthew and Mark follow the story of his bold confession of faith in Jesus as Messiah with an account of how his inability to understand the dangerousness of Jesus' mission drew from Jesus the rebuke, "Get thee behind me, Satan." His assertion in Jerusalem of his willingness, if necessary, to die with Jesus is followed in all the Gospels by the account of his denying that he had ever known Jesus. When Jesus was arrested, Peter alone had the courage to follow right into the house of the high priest, but when association with Jesus seemed likely to endanger his life, his courage failed him. We can compare these stories with Paul's experience at Antioch. At first Peter had the boldness of faith to join with Paul in disregarding Jewish food laws and in eating at a common table with uncircumcised Gentile Christians, but when a protest was made by the more conservative Jewish Christians of Jerusalem, Peter withdrew from table fellowship with the Gentile Christians and betrayed the unity of Jew and Gentile in Christ in the Antioch church. Paul told him to his face that he was failing to uphold the truth of the gospel. Acts preserves a tradition of Peter's progressiveness, making him precede all others in breaking out beyond the bounds of the Jewish community to admit a Gentile into a full participation in the church and even makes him an apostle to the Gentiles parallel with Paul, although it narrates no contact of Peter with Gentiles beyond Cornelius. Galatians 2:7 is more likely an indication of Peter's scope of mission where Paul speaks of Peter's being an apostle to the Jews who were scattered across the world while he himself was apostle to the Gentiles. Acts, strangely, after showing clearly

Peter's place of leadership in the earliest church, merely reports his departure from Jerusalem and gives no indication of the nature of his later ministry. If it were not for Paul's report of his controversy with him in Antioch and an incidental remark (I Cor. 9:5) that Peter traveled about the world in the company of his wife at the church's expense, we would know nothing of Peter's larger mission.

The realistic way in which the church remembered Peter's failures is directly in the Old Testament tradition. Except in a later version of the Davidic tradition, there was little attempt to glorify or idealize the great leaders of the past. They appear with all their warts and in all their weaknesses. Abraham, to protect his own life in Egypt, lies about his wife and endangers the whole future that has been promised him by God. Jacob, the immediate father of the twelve tribes, has few admirable traits in his character, and his sons are most of them a crude and primitive lot. David, the great king, is remembered as having been also an outlaw and a murderer. Israel had no illusions about the humanity that God had to use in the fulfillment of his purposes, nor had the early church. The disciples are remembered at their moments of ambition for precedence, their intolerance of an unauthorized exorcist, their inability to stay awake in Jesus' hour of crisis, their obtuseness to Jesus' meaning and general inability to share his spirit. But Peter, the foremost of them all, is singled out as the one who was surest of his faith and then, when the hour of testing came, failed most miserably. It is important, however, to remember that the church which heard the story of Peter's failure knew also of the recovery of his faith and of his achievements as a bold apostle. A church in which many had in some degree denied their Lord under stress of severe persecution could draw great encouragement from the account of Peter's relation with Jesus.

PETER THE REPRESENTATIVE DISCIPLE

The measure in which the church identified itself with Peter has to be kept in mind as we examine individual traditions concerning him. We can see the process at work when we compare the accounts of his call to become a disciple in Mark and Luke. In the earlier version in Mark, Peter is just one of four fishermen who respond to Jesus' invitation. But, as Luke tells the story, it becomes a dramatic experience of Peter's, with the others merely accompanying him, and an astonishing miracle calls forth the faith of Peter. In Mark there is no miracle; Jesus challenges the four to become fishers for men, that is, to share with him in his mission of redemption, and they leave their occupation to go with him. In Luke, however, Jesus, after using the fishermen's boat as a pulpit from which to teach the people on the shore, commands Peter to put out into the deep and let down his nets. Peter protests that they have been fishing all night and have caught nothing. But when he obeys the command, the nets are filled so full that they begin to break, and when the fish are transferred to the boats, the boats are so full that they begin to sink. Peter falls down then at Jesus' knees and cries out, "Depart from me, for I am a sinful man, O Lord." At this point Jesus invites him and the others to become fishers for men and they leave everything to follow him.

One suspects that Luke, who in the Acts is so careful to keep Peter and Paul parallel with each other as the two great leaders of the early church, was interested to have a call of Peter that would balance the dramatic story of the call of Paul. John, ch. 21, preserves a variant account of Peter and the others at the command of Jesus drawing in a great catch of fish, which Luke perhaps combined with Mark's tradition of the call. But Peter has now become representative of the church in confrontation with its Lord. The command to put out into the deep and let down the nets is understood as a command to put out boldly into the world and engage in mission. Peter's protest echoes the ever-renewed complaint that the effort has been fruitless. But obedience to the command in spite of the hopeless outlook brings the miracle of the catch and Peter, like the church, recognizes in it the awesome presence and power of God. Peter's words "Depart from me . . ." are meant to show that the event for him had been a revelation of God. Like Isaiah of old, he is utterly humbled and crushed as his sinfulness is revealed in the presence of God's holiness, and his humility prepares him to respond to Jesus' invitation. We may prefer Mark's simpler and less dramatic version of the call, but we can understand how Luke, with his central interest in the church's mission to the whole world and with his special interest in Peter, combined two traditions to produce his own version in which Peter is representative of the church. Luke's interest is not in the catching of fish but in the catching of men.

This representative character of Peter is even more obvious in Matthew's story of the confession at Caesarea Philippi. Jesus' questions are addressed to all the disciples. All answer the first question, but Peter alone answers the second and from that point the dialogue is solely with him. The inference has been drawn from this that Peter alone confessed Jesus as Messiah, that Peter alone of the disciples was recognized by Jesus as having received the revelation of the Father, and that to Peter alone was assigned the power of binding and loosing. Matthew 18:18, however, suggests strongly that the author of the Gospel of Matthew, for all the prominence he gave to Peter, did not think of him in these terms. The power of binding and loosing is there assigned to all the disciples. Moreover, the confession "Thou art the Christ, the Son of the living God" is the basic confession of the whole church. Neither Peter nor anyone else can know the truth of it unless it is revealed to him by the Father. And wherever that truth is known and that confession made, the church is founded on a rock. Peter as the first among equals symbolizes in his relation with Jesus the church's continuing relation with its Lord. The fact that both Mark and Matthew follow the story of the confession with the story of Jesus' rebuke to Peter would seem to show their desire to undercut any undue glorification of Peter as an individual. He who in one moment could be addressed as the impregnable rock on which the church is built is in the next moment Satan to his Lord. The church of the New Testament was not acquainted with any infallible men. Christian disciples had always two possibilities before them: they could be the light of the world or a light hidden from the world under a basin, salt of the earth or a flavorless substance from which all its salt content had been drained away, impregnable rock or agent of Satan.

There is a consistency in the representations of Peter between Caesarea Philippi and the crucifixion. He acts as a kind of foil over against which the mind and spirit of Jesus stand out more clearly. He expresses the mind of our common humanity in its contrast with the mind of Christ. This accords with Jesus' accusation against him in Matt. 16:23 that he was not on the side of God but of men. In Matt. 18:21, he is spokesman for what men through the ages have considered to be a generous practice of forgiveness. He has forgiven the brother who offended him over and over and now he wants to know when he may be done forgiving. Surely to forgive seven times is sufficiently generous. Only a limited forgiveness is comprehensible to Peter. But Jesus' demand "seventy times seven" is for an unlimited forgiveness, a forgiveness that is of the same nature as God's forgiveness that knows no limit until the evil in man is overcome. In Matt. 19:27, Peter's question, asking what reward there is to be for a disciple who has accepted poverty in order to share Jesus' mission, is the perennial human question, What is there in it for me? It stands in contrast to what every reader knows is to be Jesus' reward for his acceptance of poverty and his faithfulness in his mission— the cross! In Matt. 26:33, Peter's cocksureness of the unfailing quality of his loyalty points up his all too human ignorance of himself in contrast to Jesus' knowledge of him. In Matt. 26:40, Peter's sleeping in Gethsemane while Jesus wrestles in agony with his destiny widens still more the gulf between the most faithful and trusted disciple and his Lord. Then in the final crisis the distance becomes infinite as Jesus goes resolutely to his trial and crucifixion while Peter, after following more boldly than the others for a time, chooses safety for himself in a denial of any acquaintance with Jesus. A very human church saw itself in a very human Peter.

THE JESUS WHO DEALT WITH PETER

Our attention has been focused on Peter in his relation to Jesus, but our chief interest is in what is remembered of Jesus in his ongoing encounter with Peter. First, we are impressed by the intention of Jesus, which was fulfilled eventually, to multiply himself and his mission in such wayward human material. Judas and Peter are the only two disciples of whom we get any very clear picture and in both we see how much there was that remained resistant to Jesus' purpose and spirit throughout his lifetime. And yet from the beginning the goal of his enlistment of them as disciples was that they should share his redemptive mission with him. He was fishing for men, to draw them out of the broken sterile existence so many of them had in their self-imprisonment into the fruitful life of the Kingdom in which their new relationship with God gave them a new relation with each other and with the world, and he invited them to become fishers with him. Prophets had had disciples before. Jeremiah had his Baruch. Second Isaiah had people associated with him whom he addressed as "You who tremble at the word." John the Baptist had disciples. But none of these prophets expected their followers to become prophets like themselves. They preserved the master prophet's teaching and hoped that someday God would raise up another prophet like him. But Jesus, whose mission went far beyond that of any prophet, expected of a disciple that soon he would be active in preaching, teaching, healing, and exorcising demons. It was intrinsic to his purpose that what he was doing others could do in company with him. But in order to share in his mission they had first to share in the life that he had in God. If Jesus' preaching, teaching, healing, and exorcism had its power from the presence of God's Spirit in him, the openness of relation between him and the Father, then certainly their mission could have no effectiveness except from the same source. It is strange that the Gospels do not speak of the disciples "receiving the Spirit" until after the death and resurrection of Jesus. It is absurd to think that Jesus could fulfill his mission only in the power of the Spirit and would expect them to be effective in the same mission knowing nothing of the Spirit. Perhaps the explanation is that for them in Jesus' lifetime there was no distinction between the Spirit and Jesus himself as the source of their new life in God and of their power for mission. What they discovered after the resurrection was that the removal of Jesus of Nazareth from this world, far from interrupting their access to that source of power, actually brought the Spirit they had known in fellowship with Jesus closer to them than ever before.

The paradox of Jesus' relation with Peter is the paradox of Jesus' relation with his church not only throughout the New Testament but through all time. Jesus chooses the man in spite of all his human weaknesses and binds him to himself, in intimate personal relation with him, sharing not just his teaching but his very self, taking him into his own relation with God. Peter then in this new relation acknowledges that Jesus is none other than the Christ of God, and Jesus with joy acknowledges that Peter has begun to have under him the very rock of God. But whereas Jesus' relation with the Father is an unbroken one, Peter's is broken again and again and has to be mended. The rock is not always under Peter's feet. There are times when it seems more like sand. Peter the confessor can be swiftly replaced by Peter the tempter and the denier of his Lord. In this the story of Peter is a mirror held up to the church in which it has constantly to renew its vision of the height of its calling, into oneness with its Lord, and of the sobering reality of its performance, in contradiction to its calling. The two have to be held together. When the church sees only the intention of Jesus to share his very life and mission with his disciples and forgets the brokenness of its fulfillment of this promise, it begins to think of itself as though already it were itself the Christ; it speaks as though Peter were commissioned to take the place of Christ. But on the other hand, it is possible for the church to become the victim of a false humility, to focus too intently upon the weaknesses and failures of Peter and to be deaf to the call of Christ for disciples who will share first his life in God and then his mission. This call should meet us most forcefully in the Sacrament in which Jesus in the symbols of the bread and wine seeks to give us nothing less than himself, a share in his life and, what is inseparable from that, a share in his mission.

In Jesus' relation with Peter we see also the limitation upon what he could do directly for a disciple. He could not tell Peter

or any other person who he was. There are some scholars who
hold that Jesus had no consciousness of being the Messiah or of
standing in any unique relation between God and man, that to
himself he was just another prophet or rabbi of a distinctive
kind, heralding the approach of a day of judgment and fulfillment. But this is to credit him with a remarkable blindness to
what others were soon to see with such clarity and conviction.
Certainly he rejected the whole popular concept of a political
messiah who would subdue the nations with supernatural power.
But he consciously and deliberately claimed for his word an
authority that reached beyond the limits of the sacred Torah.
His redemptive mission was not just the heralding of a future
new age but was itself the spearhead of the invasion of the
present world by that new age. There was a mystery about his
person and the mystery was created by the relation between his
person, words and actions, and the divine power which through
him visibly transformed people's lives. There was a depth to his
existence that he could not put into words for anyone. It could
be understood by another person only as that person began to
discover in some measure the same depth of mystery in his own
existence and to draw upon it as the source of his strength and
vision.

If the gospel had been simply a new teaching, then it could
all of it have been conveyed in words and preserved intact for
future generations by being written in a book. The fact that Jesus
wrote nothing is significant. He did not trust his gospel to a set
of words because he knew that all the words could be remembered and held in honor and at the same time the reality of his
gospel be lost and forgotten. The living heart of his gospel was
hidden in the mystery of his person. His mission was not to
capture men for a new religious teaching or a new religious cult
but to open to them their only true life in God, a life in God
that was the mystery of his own being, his joy and at the same
time his burden. He could impart it to men only by giving them
himself. And what was true of his own mission would be true of
his disciples' mission: they could open the life of the Kingdom to
others only when it was the reality of their own life in God and

only when they were willing to share it in openness with others. But the ultimate reality of the life of the new age, its source and foundation, was God himself, who remains hidden from the eyes of men and in the words of men. Therefore, at the most crucial point in Jesus' relation with Peter, Jesus could not do for Peter what had to be done; he could not solve the problem of Peter's faith for him; he could not with a few well-spoken words transport him from his time of wayward and twilight faith to a time of constant and clear-sighted faith. He had first to die in faithfulness to his mission before Peter's eyes were opened to see. The mystery not only of Jesus' existence but also of Peter's existence had to be "revealed," and revelation is not at any man's disposal. Jesus himself had to wait for the Father to open Peter's eyes and let him see into the depths of the mystery of the gospel. The revelation was not apart from Jesus' words of preaching and teaching, but of themselves the words were not sufficient. No words of themselves are ever sufficient.

One aspect of Jesus' dealing with Peter which shows how Jesus dealt with his disciples is his forthrightness, one might even say severity. He does not gently suggest that Peter has not as yet grasped how dangerous their mission is but turns on him sharply with the rebuke, "Get thou behind me, Satan," and with the warning that Peter is not seeing the situation as it appears from the side of God. Similar to this is his abrupt dismissal of Peter's protestation of undying loyalty, cutting through the sentimentalism of Peter's faith to the reality of what he can expect from Peter. He knew what was in men. He read them with an astonishing accuracy because he seemed to see them always as they were before God. And this was what they were to remember—that his knowledge of them was like God's knowledge of them, seeing the whole unpalatable truth about them and yet not despairing of them. What met them in Jesus was both divine judgment and divine grace, a judgment that was as ruthless as God's and a grace and pardon that were no different from God's grace and pardon.

It is peculiar that in the Gospels, Peter has no prominence in the stories of Jesus' resurrection appearances, except in the Gospel of John where, together with the disciple whom Jesus loved, he discovered the emptiness of the tomb, and yet Paul in I Cor. 15:5 reports a church tradition that Jesus *first* appeared to Peter, then to the Twelve. This resurrection experience was decisive for Peter as it was to be later for Paul. It is not to be thought of as an event separate from all that had preceded it in the relation between Jesus and Peter but rather as the climactic point in that relation. The cross and Peter's disillusionment about his faith in the hour of crisis had broken down an inner wall of resistance and blindness. His eyes were opened to see who it was whose judgment and grace had been exerting their transforming influence upon him all this time and still continued unfailingly with him beyond the tomb. The resurrection was for Peter as for Paul the revelation of the presence and power of God in Jesus Christ and the decisive inbreaking of that power upon him to become the source of a ministry in continuity with that of Jesus himself, never completely without a brokenness and need of healing, yet fruitful in the same way that Jesus' ministry had been fruitful.

Chapter IX

JESUS AND NICODEMUS

THE ENCOUNTER OF JESUS with Nicodemus in John, ch. 3, is as different from all the others we have considered as the Gospel of John is different from the other Gospels. Instead of a clear-cut dialogue with a beginning and an ending, we have a dialogue that gradually becomes a monologue and Nicodemus seems just to fade out of the picture to reappear briefly twice in later chapters. Even in the dialogue Nicodemus is very much a stylized figure rather than a man of flesh and blood: he never does get his question asked before Jesus puzzles him with an ultimatum; he then merely exclaims how incredible it is to him that a man should be born again, and his exclamations draw forth extensions of Jesus' teaching. He is little more than a foil for a development of Christian doctrine and yet there are points of similarity between this encounter and the others. Nicodemus begins to have something in common with the other figures in the way in which he represents a form of Pharisaism, in this instance one that could be respectful to Jesus without understanding him. The author of the Gospel has been building up the contrast between the old and the new, between the Torah of Moses and the word of Christ, between the prophet John and the Lamb of God, between the water of Judaism and the wine of the gospel, between the old temple of perishable stone and the new imperishable temple of the Spirit. In Nicodemus he sets the Pharisaism of the synagogue in contrast with the new existence men know as children of God in the church. As C. K. Barrett[30] says in his commentary on the Gospel of John: "We are made to hear not a conversation between two persons but the dialogue of church and synagogue in which (according to the Christian view) the former completes and fulfils the latter, which is in consequence superseded." Barrett finds the representative character of Nicodemus evident also in the piling up of titles and in the way in which Nicodemus, in using the plural "we," speaks for more than himself, perhaps for the "many" of John 2:23.

The feature of the encounter that is most reminiscent of the other encounters is the abruptness of Jesus, making no response to Nicodemus' polite and complimentary approach, but with one stroke cutting through to the heart of the man's problem. It was a kind of shock treatment. While the inquirer was feeling his way cautiously toward what he expected to be an enriching conversation with Jesus, Jesus with his knowledge of the Pharisee mentality and the way in which it unconsciously used religion as a protection against God's ultimate and unconditional claim upon man, gave the encounter a fresh beginning by confronting the Pharisee with God's claim. To Nicodemus it was to be a conversation between an earnest religious inquirer who held an honored place in the religious community and an impressive new teacher who had validated his legitimacy by the works he had already accomplished. But Jesus was unwilling to accept that conception of their relation. To him there was a vast gulf between himself and Nicodemus, as wide as the gulf between heaven and earth. He spoke from within the new age, the Kingdom of God, while Nicodemus stood firmly rooted in the old age which in spite of all its religion and morality was blind to the reality of the new age. Nicodemus still lives in the world of flesh and cannot see beyond his world of flesh to the world of Spirit that is dawning upon mankind in the mission of Jesus. The language that is used here, such as the contrast between flesh and spirit, is undoubtedly the language of the author of the Gospel of John just as throughout the Gospel we find him using a terminology that belongs to a time and place other than that of Jesus as he reinterprets the gospel for a new constituency, but the figure and stance of Jesus is recognizably that which we have seen in his encounters with Simon the Pharisee and with the man of wealth.

The contrast between the life of flesh and the new life as a child of God under God's sovereignty occurs also both in the Pauline letters and in the other Gospels. Paul was to give classic expression to this basic antithesis in his doctrine of the two ages, the old age under the law which had no future but frustration and death, and the new age of the Spirit inaugurated by Christ in his death and resurrection in which grace and truth reign supreme and life moves steadily toward its fulfillment in the Parousia. For Paul, the death of Jesus was the end of the old age and its religious structures in the sense that it revealed its ultimate contradiction to God's purpose and its alienation from God, and his resurrection was the unveiling of Christ reigning as Lord over the life of the new age, the hidden center and source of its existence. To pass from the old to the new, one had to die with Christ and rise with him into a new self and a new creation, but Paul makes very plain that decisive as the beginning may be, the Christian never completes the transition from the old to the new within the span of his lifetime.

The Gospel of John expresses the transition in terms of a rebirth. A man is born in a fleshly way into the world of flesh, but if he is ever to enter upon his true life as a child of God and know the life of the Kingdom, there has to be a second beginning which is described as "born again," "born of the Spirit," "born of God." These terms have long been commandeered by evangelists who have equated rebirth with a sudden highly emotional decision that is evoked by evangelistic preaching. It is difficult to get the words free from that association and to recover the meaning that the Gospel of John intended, but it is certainly very close to what Paul expressed in different terms. The old self, however religious and moral it may be, is blind to its true life in God. No man is truly himself, the man whom God created him to be, until his whole existence has its center beyond himself in God. Jesus is the revelation of what human life can be when it is wholly indwelt by the Word and Spirit of God. But he came not to have that life in himself alone but to impart it to all men.

He knew himself to be the Son of the Father and had as his mission that all men might become sons, children of the Father, together with him. To be born again was thus to enter upon a relation with God like Jesus' own relation with the Father. It is not just a single sudden experience but a relation that encompasses the whole of life.

In the Synoptic Gospels Jesus does not use the language of rebirth or of dying and rising, but speaks only of "becoming as little children with God." The break between the old world and the new, the old self and the new, is expressed in his demand for repentance, a word for which the Gospel of John has little use. But no one was left long in doubt that the new age meant new attitudes and a new outlook upon almost everything in life. And behind the attitudes and outlook was a new relation with God. Jesus' diagnosis of the source of man's helplessness and failure was a rupture in his relationship with God at the center of his life. A man might believe in God and try most devotedly to obey his commands but he was serving an absent rather than a present God. What he did not know was the reality of God with him. Reaching for a God somewhere in the beyond, he missed him in the here and now and failed to stand before him in the here and now. "The Kingdom of God at hand" in Jesus' message meant "God here and now." This was what made all the difference, no longer to be reaching toward a distant God but to be living joyfully out of resources of strength and love and understanding in a present God. To be as a child with the Father was to be no longer at the mercy of hostile forces in an alien world but able to face even the harshest experiences of life with a confidence that somehow they would be made eventually to serve a Father's purpose. But the depiction of the disciples in the Synoptic Gospels does not suggest at all that the realization of their relation of sonship with the Father (which is parallel to and synonymous with "born of God") was fully accomplished in the moment of their decision to respond to the gospel in repentance and faith and to become disciples.

Setting forth these parallels gives support to the view that in spite of the differences in the Johannine terminology and the distinctly representative character of the figure of Nicodemus, the passage preserves a valid memory of what it was like for Jesus to encounter a very earnest and respectable Pharisee. Here as elsewhere the author has dealt with the traditional material with great freedom but not irresponsibly. There is at the heart of the dialogue a memory of what it was like to be confronted by Jesus and to be claimed by him for the life of his Kingdom.

The bluntness of Jesus in dealing with Nicodemus must not be allowed to conceal the fact that the author of the Gospel intends us to have a sympathetic impression of Nicodemus. He is a distinguished representative of Pharisaism, a teacher of religion himself and a member of the Sanhedrin. We have to dismiss from our minds the popular misconception of the Pharisees which, on the basis of some of Jesus' harsh words concerning them, portrays them as invariably hypocritical, small-minded, self-righteous, boastful. They were actually the most progressive religious force in Judaism, the backbone of synagogue worship and the guardians of the moral and religious life of the community. They studied the Scriptures diligently themselves and taught them to others. The New Testament shows us different types. Some, like Simon who entertained Jesus at supper, were merely curious about Jesus and coldly critical of him. Others, like the pre-Christian Paul, saw in Jesus and his followers a threat to the established religious structures that should not be tolerated for a moment. Gamaliel in Acts speaks for a more liberal and tolerant Pharisaism which was content to wait and see what would come of the movement. But Nicodemus speaks for a type of Pharisee who was deeply impressed by Jesus' achievements and sincerely interested to learn from him. That he exercised caution on his first visit, coming by night in order to escape observation by his more hostile colleagues, is only to be expected and should not be held against him. He had the courage later to protest in the Sanhedrin against Jesus' being condemned without being heard (John 7:50–51) and, after Jesus' death, to provide materials for the embalming of the body (John 19:39). The latter action suggests that he was a man of considerable wealth. In fact, the more completely we etch the features of Nicodemus, the more like he becomes to the respectful and inquiring man of wealth in Mark 10:17 ff. Just as that man began his conversation with Jesus with the complimentary "Good Master," so Nicodemus begins by assuring Jesus that he recognizes him as a teacher sent from God. And just as Jesus met the compliment with a rebuke, so here there are no civilities but instead the shock of an ultimatum.

NICODEMUS AS A CHRISTIAN TYPE

We begin to see the significance of this encounter of Jesus with Nicodemus only when for us Nicodemus ceases to be representative merely of the religion of the synagogue at its best and becomes representative of all religion and morality, whether Christian, Jewish, or any other. What more could even a Christian church ask of a man than what we see in Nicodemus? A firm believer in God, a student of the Scriptures, a diligent participant in worship, a teacher of religion, a responsible member of the governing body of the community, and in contrast to some of his more proud and arrogant colleagues, a man humble in confrontation with Jesus and with an eagerness to learn from him. Yet Jesus consigned all of this to the world of the "flesh," separated by a great gulf from the world of the Spirit, the Kingdom of God! We have to remove from our minds any equation of "flesh" with evil. "Flesh" in the Gospel of John, as in the letters of Paul, denotes primarily the world insofar as man is central and sovereign in it. "Flesh" for the Hebrews included the whole life of man, not just its physical and material aspects but the intellectual and spiritual as well. Man is flesh and God is spirit. But for Jesus, as for the author of the Gospel of John and for Paul, the world of the flesh is being invaded by the Spirit of God and a totally new possibility of life for man is being opened to him. This is the uniquely new element in the gospel that makes its proclamation the time of fulfillment in relation to the time of promise represented by the whole Old Testament. It was this, as we saw earlier, that distinguished the mission and person of Jesus from the mission and person of John the Baptist. It is this which has made the pitifully brief and meagerly successful ministry of Jesus the turning point in human history. The flesh of man is invaded, conquered, and transformed by the present indwelling Spirit of God and in the transformation man becomes truly man.

The tragedy of Christianity is that it constantly loses sight of what is unique and revolutionary in the gospel, ceases to think in terms of a divine invasion of our human world, and makes of itself merely the purest and noblest of all religions. It expects of its adherents somewhat less than Nicodemus expected of himself. Belief in God, a reasonably moral life, loyalty to the church and its programs, together with some sense of social responsibility, is sufficient. If Jesus is regarded as divine, it is entirely a matter of his personal status and has nothing whatever to do with the presence and action of God's Spirit in him which he expected to continue in all those who became bonded together with him in faith and to be the determining reality in their existences. The Holy Spirit no longer has any clear or certain meaning for most members of the church, a vaguely pervasive spiritual influence perhaps, not closely identified with the Jesus of the Gospels, a mystifying third element in the Trinity. That the uniqueness of the gospel is inseparable from the reality denoted by this word "Spirit" and is lost from sight when the Spirit is lost from sight is rarely glimpsed. But we must see that insofar as Christianity lets itself become merely another form of religion and morality, it takes its stand alongside Nicodemus. Like Nicodemus, it is bewildered by everything the New Testament says about being "born of the Spirit" or "indwelt by the Spirit." Because this happens so often and, in its happening, the religion of Christians becomes remarkably similar to the religion of the Pharisees, at least at some points, it becomes not only possible but necessary for Christians to see themselves in Nicodeumus and in other Pharisees in their confrontation with Jesus. We may even venture the generalization that there is a tendency in all forms of Christianity in the course of time to take on something of the spirit and character of Pharisaism.

This reduction of Christianity, from a movement of the Spirit of God that brings man to the fulfillment of his human existence and therefore lays claim upon all mankind, to just one religion among the religions of man, to us the most superior, has had strong support in modern times both in the general world of culture and among theologians. There has seemed to be a narrowness and arrogance and also an intellectual blindness, in the posture of Christians who set the Christian faith in a class by itself beyond all other religions and take literally the Johannine statement that Jesus Christ is *the* truth. An objective comparison of the phenomena of religion in the history of Bible and church and in the history of other religions produces too many parallels, turns up too many impressive features in the other religions, and discloses too many perverse and wayward developments in Christian history for Christians to make such extravagant claims for their faith. A more modest attitude seems appropriate to the facts: the Christian should come down from his lofty perch, let his religion take its place among the multiple religions of man and surrender both the claim to universality and the missionary enterprise that goes with it. The appeal of this attitude is very strong. And nowhere is the pressure of it felt more keenly than when we come into intimate relation with our brothers of the Jewish faith, especially when, like Nicodemus, they are ready to recognize in Jesus one of the greatest among all the great Jewish teachers of religion. We would not dare to say to them, as Jesus said to Nicodemus, "Unless you are born of the Spirit, you cannot see the Kingdom of God." We would not dare to say it because there is not the same gulf or tension between our Christian religion and their Jewish religion that there was between the original Christian movement and the religion of the synagogue. For Jesus, the gulf was so deep and the tension so great that it imperilled his life. For Paul, it was a gulf between two ages. He knew the values of the religion and culture in which he had grown up, but they seemed as nothing in comparison with the life that became his in Christ. But today the gulf seems little more than a gully and all reason for tension seems to have vanished. From one aspect this may be seen as a sign of humility on the part of modern Christians, divesting themselves of self-righteousness and recognizing how much they have in common with

Judaism. But from another aspect it is disturbing as a sign of the extent to which Christians have lost sight of what was originally most distinctive and unique in the Christian gospel, in short, that which made Jesus and Paul rebels against the established religion of their time. If they were honest with themselves, they would have to admit that they are best content with a religion roughly similar to that of Nicodemus and not at all interested in being born of the Spirit into Jesus' new age of the Kingdom.

BORN OF THE SPIRIT

If we are to understand what Jesus was asking of Nicodemus, and expects also of us if we are to call ourselves Christians with some validity, we need to delve more deeply behind the phrase "born of the Spirit" or "born of God." The language of rebirth occurs not only in later New Testament documents, primarily in the Johannine Gospel and letters (I John 2:29; 3:9; 4:7; 5:1, 18), but also in Titus 3:5 and I Peter 1:3,23. As we have seen, Paul prefers to speak of the Christian's dying to the old world and rising into a new world with Christ. In the Synoptic Gospels a very close parallel to the saying in John 3:3 and 5 and most likely the original saying of Jesus is, "Except you become as little children you shall not enter into the Kingdom of God." Joachim Jeremias tells us that Jesus' use of "Abba" in address-ing God in prayer was unusual. In contemporary Jewish prayers no such word was used. It is the child's name for his father and Jesus, in using it, gives expression to what is for him the only possible relation for a human being with God, as a child with his father. There is always a danger of these terms being senti-mentalized by us. In the Jewish context the word "Father" ex-pressed much more of sovereignty, initiative, and authority than it does with us, and to Jesus to be a child of God was to be obedient to his rule, unfailingly responsive to his guidance, and confident of his wisdom even when his ways were hard to under-stand. But it was much more than this. When he rebuked the disciples for their rivalry concerning precedence and contrasted their spirit with the spirit of a child, what troubled him was not just the contention that was disrupting their relations with each other but the absence in them of the childlike spirit that would be evidence of a right relation with God. In the Beatitudes, Jesus called this spirit "meekness," not what currently passes as meekness, which is closer to servility, but a meekness like his own, which was a radical humbling of the human self before God that produced an openness and responsiveness not only to God but to every human being. The enemy of this openness and responsiveness was man's ego-centeredness, his unconscious assumption that first place in his world should belong to him, and, even in his religion, the subtle reversal of order in his relation with God that made God subordinate to his purposes. Hence the necessity of a radical repentance or turning round of man's existence for him to be a child with God. The essential sin, or sickness, of man as Jesus considered it was his imprisonment within himself, his enslavement to his own self-will, which blinded him both to God and to his fellowman. And how very effectively the self-centered man could use his religion and morality, his prayers to God and his deeds of charity, to bolster his self-justification, to assure himself concerning his relation with God and so to resist the ultimate claim of God upon him, Jesus knew only too well! It meant a serious humbling of proud humanity, especially of proud religious and moral humanity, to become as a child with God.

There are a number of other terms that the church used to describe Jesus' relation with God that may throw some light upon this point of ultimate mystery. That Jesus is Son of God and Christians sons of God through their faith in him is directly parallel with "child of God" and "children of God." But so also is "image of God" a synonym for "Son of God," and to be "children of God" is to be like God (Matt. 5:45). In the same way Jesus can speak of himself as "servant" and of his disciples as "servants," and Paul can make "servant" his proudest title as an apostle. Compare with all of these the way in which in the story of Jesus' birth in Luke 1:35 Jesus is conceived by the Holy Spirit, which means that from the first moment of his human existence he was wholly "born of the Spirit," and then

through faith in him Christians come to be "born of the Spirit."
Each of these pairs of terms is an expression of one and the
same reality, so that they interpret each other mutually and the
two halves of each pair must be understood together. For instance, the title "Son of God" takes on a different shade of
meaning when behind it we see Jesus' understanding of himself
as a child of the Father and this in turn is deepened by the recognition that a personal relation with God has reality only when
the very nature of God is imaged or reflected in the human
partner, and that so immediate is the presence of God in this
relation that it can best be conceived as an indwelling Spirit. But
when we hold together the two halves of each pair of terms, we
begin to see how the existence of a Christian is defined and determined by the existence of Jesus Christ. To be a Christian is
nothing less than to be taken into Jesus' own relation with God,
and the mission of Jesus, which became the mission of the
church, is to share with all men the joy and strength and health
of his own life in God. He was Son of God that all men might
be sons of God. He was as a child of God that all men might
find the one true basis of their life in being children of the one
God and members together in his family. This immediacy of
relation was the new covenant relation into which he sought to
draw all men and in which the will of God was no longer im-
posed from without but was written on men's hearts from within.
He came not to found a new religion but to set God in men's
hearts and he could give them God only by giving them himself.
But his very self was not just the man Jesus from Nazareth but
the Spirit of God which made him what he was in himself and in
his mission.

To be born of the Spirit is thus to participate in Jesus' own
relation with God and to have our life shaped and determined
from within by the same immediate presence of God. The terms
"servant" and "servants" against their Old Testament background have a double significance. On the one hand, they de-
note the radical binding of the human will to God's will. "Servant" may be translated "slave," "slave of God." The servant

is unconditionally at the disposal of God's purpose in the world. But in the ancient world it was the prime minister of the king who was called his "servant," and in Second Isaiah, as well as elsewhere in the Old Testament, the servant of God is the cherished representative of God in the midst of human history through whom God is working out his redemptive purpose for all mankind. It was Second Isaiah who, six centuries before the time of Jesus, recognized so clearly how dangerous it was to stand in such an intimate relation with God. To be a child of God suggests security. To be filled with God's Spirit suggests power. But neither the security nor the power are of a kind that provides safety in the world. The servant of God who in his intimate relation with God has reflected in him the compassion of God for the poor and oppressed, the hatred of God for cruelty and injustice, the truth of God that cannot endure lies, and the determination of God that men should be free from bondage finds himself confronted with an established order in the world that is in sharpest contradiction to the mind of God. Therefore, it is a costly thing to be filled with the Spirit of God and to be a child of God. Far too often these terms concerning the Spirit have been allowed to suggest some kind of inner mystical experience. The same is true of Paul's favorite expressions "in Christ" and "Christ in me." But in the New Testament being filled with the Spirit is not a mystic experience that is attained in withdrawal from the world but, rather, a very practical and concrete employment in God's service in the community, and for Paul to have Christ in him expresses his consciousness of the mission of Jesus Christ being reproduced in his own mission. There is no other Spirit known in the New Testament except the Spirit that empowered Jesus for his mission and it was inconceivable that anyone should receive the Spirit or be born of the Spirit and not be empowered and equipped for participation in the same mission. The question, therefore, with which Jesus confronted Nicodemus, and with which he also confronts us, is whether we are interested only in the maintenance and improvement of our religion or whether we are willing to embark with him on God's great redemptive enterprise, the coming of the new age in which men as children of God find what it is to be really human and share what they find with their fellowmen.

BUT HOW IS ONE BORN OF GOD?

The one question that remains is Nicodemus' "How?" and the answer that Jesus gives has often seemed to be much vaguer than it really is—through a misinterpretation. The words concerning the wind (the same word means both "wind" and "spirit") blowing where it will and that you hear the sound of it but know neither where it comes from nor whither it goes, then the assertion, "So is it with everyone who is born of the Spirit," have been understood as though the answer to "how" were left hanging in the air, as though it were always a complete mystery how anyone is born of the Spirit. The likening of the Spirit to the wind which has such unseen power and yet whose movements are beyond man's comprehension or control does speak of the mystery of God's presence. But the wind has a voice, and so also does the Spirit of God have a voice that can be heard. Spirit and Word are always held together in the Gospel of John. There is no Spirit without the Word and the Spirit in the Word is God himself in his Word. The word of the Gospel cannot be truly heard until, in the hearing, God himself in his Spirit is received into one's life. The voice of the Spirit is the Word, and the Spirit is given in the hearing of the Word. We need also to understand why in John 3:5 the text says "born of water and the Spirit." This has sometimes been taken to mean that baptism was necessary for the receiving of the Spirit. But it seems more likely that the author of John's Gospel was seeking to combat the idea current in his church that baptism with water would be sufficient to make a man a Christian. There were many pagan influences in the first-century world to encourage the superstitious idea of baptismal regeneration. Paul made it his general principle, to which he permitted few exceptions, not to baptize anyone, in order to combat this misconception. For him it was in the preaching of Christ crucified and risen that the Spirit was given. It is noteworthy that in John 4:2 Jesus too is said not to have baptized his converts. Baptism with water was insufficient for regeneration. There had to be a receiving of the Spirit and the Spirit could be known only in the hearing of God's voice in the Word. The answer, therefore, to Nicodemus' question, "How?" was the word that was already sounding in his ears, the word that was incarnate in the person standing there before him. The Spirit might be mysteriously unseen but the Spirit had a human voice, in fact had had a human voice through the ages whenever men had ears to hear it, and the destiny of men depended upon their hearing and responding to that voice.

Chapter X

JESUS AND PAUL

IT MAY SEEM NAÏVE to include in this series of encounters in which the church remembered Jesus the story of Paul's conversion as it is told in Acts, chs. 9; 22; and 26. The objection might well be made that, whereas the preceding nine encounters are clearly with the Jesus of history, this one is clearly with the Christ of faith. But that is to assume a separation between the Jesus of history and the Christ of faith in the mind and tradition of the church which is not at all immediately apparent. All the encounters we have studied were for the church encounters with the Christ of faith. Just as the line between Peter and the church or between Nicodemus and the synagogue becomes dim, the person confronting Jesus in the dialogue taking on a representative character that reaches far forward, so also the line between the Jesus of history and the Christ of faith becomes dim. The Jesus who astounds Peter in the story of his call in Luke, ch. 5, is not readily distinguishable from the Jesus who commissions Peter to feed his sheep in John, ch. 21, and in turn the Jesus of this latter story is not too far removed from the risen Lord in Paul's conversion. All are, for the church, significant instances of confrontation with Jesus Christ and all bear the marks of having been reshaped to some extent in the church's memory and transmission of them. This reshaping in the mind of the church may trouble some people, suggesting to them that the stories as we have them are not an immediate unaltered transcript of the experiences as they actually occurred. On the contrary, the marks of such reshaping should reassure us that the stories are not inventions but genuine memories, because this is the way in which memory works, especially the memory of a community preserving the stories that relate to its origin.

The story of Paul's conversion, like the other stories, comes to us from a church tradition. This needs to be emphasized because the assumption is frequently made that we have the story directly from Paul by way of his friend Luke. The argument is that the book of Acts was written by Luke, a companion of Paul on his final voyage from Greece to Palestine and then when he went as a prisoner to Rome, so that everything concerning Paul in it is firsthand information. This is a theory which is not supported by the evidence but, rather, is contradicted by it. A travel diary by a companion of Paul is incorporated in Acts, but the author of Luke-Acts makes a practice of rewriting his source material to such a degree that one cannot argue, as Harnack and others have done, from the similarity of language in the travel document and the remainder of the book that the companion of Paul was the author of the whole of Luke-Acts. There are serious contrasts and contradictions between Paul as he is represented in Acts and Paul as he presents himself to us in his letters. The gospel he preaches in Acts is not identical with the gospel he affirms in his letters. The story of his movements following his conversion in Acts, ch. 9, is in direct contradiction to what he himself tells us in Galatians. Acts subordinates him to the Jerusalem apostles and withholds from him an apostolic status parallel with theirs, while Paul in his letters insists vehemently that he is in no way inferior to them as an apostolic witness. The outcome of the Jerusalem consultation is reported differently by Paul and by the author of Acts.

If this were not sufficient, then there are in the three accounts of Paul's conversion in Acts variations that are incomprehensible if the author had the story directly from Paul's lips but quite comprehensible if he was dependent upon church tradition. In all three there is evidence of the externalization of the elements of a visionary experience which frequently happens as a story of this kind is retold. The prophet Isaiah in narrating his vision is describing what he alone would see and hear that day in the Temple, but had the report come to us not directly from him but through the medium of the community's tradition, the shaking of the threshold, the smoke that filled the Temple, and other elements of the vision would likely have been reported as though they were outwardly observable by anyone who happened to be present. This has happened in the accounts of the descent of the Spirit at Jesus' baptism. What can only have been an event in Jesus' experience is progressively externalized until in the Fourth Gospel it becomes the movement of a bird earthward, observed by the prophet John. Similarly, in the stories of Paul's conversion, elements of what was in its intrinsic nature Paul's vision of the risen Lord are made visible or audible to the people who were with him. In Acts, ch. 9, they hear the voice of Christ but see nothing. In Acts, ch. 22 and ch. 26, they see the blinding light but hear nothing. Anyone who is familiar with what happens in oral transmission recognizes at once that the author of Acts has drawn his stories from church traditions and not directly from Paul. This recognition then places the encounter in the same category as the other encounters with which we have been dealing, representative persons confronted with Jesus Christ.

It is perhaps significant that Paul himself nowhere in his letters narrates directly the story of his conversion. The type of preaching that seeks to generate conversions by telling stories of conversion actually can draw no encouragement from the example of Paul. In Gal. 1:16 where alone in his letter he refers directly to his conversion he says very simply that God "was pleased to reveal his Son in me." And in II Cor., ch. 12, where he describes a visionary experience of Christ, "caught up to the third heaven . . . into Paradise . . . and heard things that cannot be told, which man may not utter," an experience that is frequently identified as his conversion, he shows an extreme reticence and attributes it to "a man in Christ" instead of making it a directly autobiographical narrative. But these passages, together with others, assure us that the central features of the encounter as described in Acts are in keeping with what we know of Paul from his letters. From II Cor. 12:7, where he speaks of an "abundance of revelations," and from I Cor. 14:18, where he confesses that speaking in tongues has a considerable place in his private devotions, we know that he was an ecstatic who had "visions of the Lord" more than once. Paul himself uses the term "visions" without any fear of thereby discounting the objectivity of what encountered him in the vision. From II Cor. 12:9 we learn that on one occasion he heard specific words of Christ in his vision which were the answer to the problem that troubled him. But Paul did not preach his visions. He was driven to write of them in his letter to Corinth only because some people in the Corinthian church were demeaning him and questioning his authority as an apostolic witness to Jesus Christ. He would have feared that in making his experiences central he would divert the focus of the gospel from Christ crucified and risen to himself. There is, then, good reason for confidence in the account of Paul's conversion in Acts, and certainly the representation of him as a passionate persecutor of the Christian movement suddenly transformed into an apostle by a vision of the risen Lord tallies with what he tells us of himself in Gal. 1:11–16 and I Cor. 15:8–10. We can accept the story as essentially accurate while recognizing that it comes to us most likely from the traditions of the Jerusalem church, colored in its details by the attitudes prevalent in that church. In fact, we may draw some reassurance from these phenomena that while the tradition might undergo some reshaping in its details through the influence of its environment, the memory of the church was remarkably faithful in the preservation of the essentials of the story.

THE CHRIST OF PAUL AND JESUS OF NAZARETH

Paul's experience has all the marks of a theophany and can best be understood when it is set in the context of Biblical theophanies. "Light" and "fire" are terms commonly used to describe the divine presence. God dwells in a light whereunto no man may approach. God appears to Moses as a blazing fire and his voice is heard from the midst of the fire. Ezekiel's vision of

God centers upon a fiery presence from which a brilliant light
shines. It is in line with these manifestations that what Paul saw
was a blinding light. There is no suggestion that he saw anything
of the figure of Jesus. His recognition of who was there before
him was entirely from the voice that spoke to him out of the
light. The light is represented as so overpowering that it blinded
him and threw him to the ground. He was in the presence of
God. But the voice that rang in his ears identified the presence
of God with the presence of none other than the Jesus of the
Christians whom he was persecuting. The voice out of the light
should for a Hebrew have been the voice of the God of Israel,
but from this time forward Paul was to assert that the voice of
Jesus Christ sounding in the ears of men was one with the voice
of the God of Israel. Indeed, he was sure that until one heard
the voice to which the Christians had responded it was impossible to hear rightly the voice of the God of Israel to which the
Scriptures bore witness.

The whole experience of his conversion Paul described very
simply in Galatians as God's revealing of his Son "in me." This
"in me" of the initial experience corresponds with the "Christ in
me" of his continuing experience. And what is signified is not
just isolated ecstatic experiences such as he describes in II Cor.,
ch. 12, but rather the personal relationship with God in and
through Jesus Christ which was established at his conversion
and was the foundation of his whole existence from that time on.
Neither for him nor for anyone else was any form of existence
any longer worthy of the name "life" except life "in Christ."
Whether he said "in Christ" or "Christ in me" he was describing
not a mystic experience to be enjoyed from time to time but the
shape of a Christian's daily existence. The life in God that was
the daily life of Jesus of Nazareth is shared with the believer.
He is taken into the mystery of the relationship of sonship in
which his whole existence is transformed by the immediacy of
God's presence. He is a new creature in a new world by the
grace of God. But this new existence is dependent upon the
bonding together of his life with the life of Jesus. Just as for
Jesus the relation with God could be expressed in differing terms

—Son of God, child of the Father, image of God, servant of a Sovereign, filled with the Spirit, the incarnate Word—so with Paul a similar set of terms can be used as in Eph. 3:16–19: "Strengthened with might through his Spirit in the inner man, that Christ may dwell in your hearts through faith, . . . being rooted and grounded in love . . . you may know the love of Christ which surpasses knowledge, that you may be filled with all the fullness of God." It is surely clear that if, as all four Gospels witness, the purpose of Jesus was to share with men his own relationship with God and to set the living, present God at the center of men's lives, thereby making them citizens of a new age in the life of humanity, he succeeded magnificently and radically in the life of this one man, Paul, in the encounter on the Damascus road. Without ever having met Paul in the flesh, Jesus did for him what he had been seeking to do with all his disciples.

It can be seen quite clearly that how we interpret the encounter of Paul with Jesus has very great significance for the question of the relation between the Jesus of history and the Christ of faith. Of course, there is no problem for those who assume that Paul had had some contact with Jesus before the crucifixion. They argue that II Cor. 5:16, "though we once knew Christ after the flesh, we no longer know him in that way," predicates some such human contact, and that the resurrection vision had its content from this previous encounter. But the passage, taken in its context, is concerned to contrast two ways of knowing, one by purely human means, the other by divine revelation, rather than two forms of contact with Christ by Paul. Added to this are three facts: that neither in Paul's letters nor in Acts is there any passage which suggests the slightest relation between Paul and Jesus in Jesus' lifetime, that Paul never refers to any events in Jesus' ministry except his institution of the Lord's Supper and his crucifixion, and that the language of Paul's gospel is quite different from the language of Jesus which meets us in the Synoptic Gospels. So strong is the evidence that Paul had never met the Jesus of history that some scholars, such as William Wrede,[31] have asserted that he knew nothing of Jesus and was unconcerned to know anything of him, that his faith and his gospel were based wholly upon the risen Christ who for him was a purely celestial being, closer to the Redeemer Lord of Gnosticism than to the Jesus of the first Christians. The Christian movement, according to this view, had two beginnings: one with Jesus which established an essentially Jewish prophetic-minded community that lived in expectation of his return at any moment as the Messiah, but a second with Paul that transformed the Jewish eschatological community into a Hellenistic religious cult with its faith centered upon a divine Lord who was already present. The only point of continuity between the Jesus of the first Christians and the Christ of Paul seemed to be the crucifixion, but even this connection was dissolved by claiming that for Paul what happened at the cross belonged in the transcendent realm of divine action rather than on the plane of human history.

Without positing any preresurrection encounter between Paul and Jesus, it does, however, seem not only possible but likely that he had some very definite knowledge of Jesus' ministry and teaching before his conversion. Paul was too intelligent a man and too deeply consecrated in his Jewish faith to become a persecutor of the Christian movement without first investigating it. He tells us in Gal. 1:14–15 that before ever he became a Christian he was conscious of having been set apart by God from his mother's womb, like Jeremiah, and knew himself called specially into the service of God. He was more zealous than any of his contemporaries for the traditions of his Jewish faith and more determined than any to protect it against such forces as threatened its dissolution. We must, therefore, ask by what process Paul arrived at the conviction that the movement originating with Jesus was a threat to the established Jewish religion as he knew it and revered it. The Jewish religious community was remarkably tolerant of variations. Pharisee and Sadducee differed widely in their concepts of Scripture, in their attitudes to the law, and in their beliefs concerning life beyond death. The Pharisees in turn were divided into conservative and liberal wings, and each of these was divided again by variations. Then there was the separatist priestly community at Qumran that had its own distinctive teachings and practices with which groups beyond Qumran were in sympathy. John the Baptist had begun a new prophetic movement with a novel practice of baptism and had been harshly critical of both Pharisees and Sadducees, yet there is no sign that either he or any of his followers were ever persecuted. Why, then, was not the movement begun by Jesus, whose members remained intensely loyal Jews even after Jesus' crucifixion, seen in parallel with John's movement and allowed to become just another variant stream within the Jewish religious community? How and why did Paul single it out as a dangerous religious and political force and decide that it should be exterminated?

Paul as a Christian grasped the revolutionary character of the gospel in a way far beyond any of those who had been with Jesus during his ministry—except perhaps Judas, as we have earlier suggested. For him, Christ was "the end of the law," that is, he brought to a conclusion the era in which Judaism on the basis of law sought to establish for men a right relation with God. There could be no compromise between a Judaism in which men could on the basis of Scripture and tradition claim for themselves a righteousness in God's sight and a Christian faith in which all men alike were sinners without excuse before God, and all alike, Jew and Gentile, could be accepted as righteous by God when in union with Christ they came to share in his righteousness, which was the life of the new age. Peter at Antioch might compromise with the traditions of Judaism when he was criticized for eating with Gentile Christians contrary to the Jewish food laws, but not Paul. And other Christians, far more passionately Jewish than Peter, insisted that no one was rightly a follower of Jesus unless, like Jesus, he received the circumcision that was the distinctive mark of the Jew. Jewish religious conservatism, intensified by nationalism, was a seriously disturbing factor in the life of the church in its early stages and threatened to make of Christianity merely a Jewish sect. But for Paul this was a betrayal of "the truth of the gospel" (Gal. 2:14). With Jesus a new era had dawned in which there was no longer Jew or Greek but all were children together in one universal family of God. The exclusiveness of Judaism belonged to the age that

had exposed its own blindness and pronounced its own doom
when it crucified the Lord of glory. Paul saw his years as a devoted Pharisee and his life as a Christian not as two stages in
religious development but as two contrasted and contradictory
eras. His passage from the one to the other he saw as death to
an old world and resurrection into a new world and a new self.
And it was this conviction of the absolute uniqueness and new-
ness of what had come into the world with Jesus Christ which
made his gospel a revolutionary force, not just in the Jewish
milieu, but in the Gentile world as well.

Is it not logical, then, to assume that what made Paul at first
a persecutor of Christians was identical with what later made
him a Christian revolutionary who was himself persecuted? Both
as a Pharisee and as a Christian he had eyes to see how radically
Jesus' gospel and practices set in question the whole existing
order of life and called for nothing less than a new beginning
with God. That he persecuted followers of Jesus and not followers of John the Baptist indicates that he recognized the radical element in Jesus' mission which, in spite of all similarities,
distinguished it from John's mission. But that would be impossible unless he had taken the trouble to learn quite definitely
what Jesus' mission and teaching were about and had as their
basic intent. Superficial impressions of the Christian movement
would never have made Paul a persecutor.

It follows also that if he "persecuted the church of God vio-
lently and tried to destroy it," as he himself says (Gal. 1:13),
he would be brought into close contact with members of the
church. From what we know of them from the New Testament,
Christians were not noted for their silence when their faith was
attacked. Surely Paul must have learned something from them
about the character of the gospel to which they were committed.
Would none of them make any attempt to persuade him of its
truth? Paul must also have known that the Christians were
claiming that their Master had risen from the dead and was
thereby revealed to be the promised Messiah of Israel and the
world, but this would be to him, it had to be, a monstrous lie

that they were telling to escape the humiliation of his execution, and therefore proof of the dishonesty of these people. If their claim were valid, then this poor little community of Christians would have to be recognized as the Israel of the Messiah to which every true Israelite would have to give his allegiance even if it meant breaking with the most cherished associations of the past. That could not be, and since it could not be, they had to be exterminated as a perversion and falsification of Israel's most sacred hope. There is no indication anywhere that Paul ever softened in his attitude toward the Christians or found himself wavering between the new faith and his inherited Pharisaism. The words of Jesus, "It hurts you to kick against the goads," which are preserved only in the third account of the conversion in Acts 26:14, if they belong to the original encounter suggest no more than that Paul had been hard pressed to maintain his position against the assault that the Christians made upon it and not at all, as some have alleged, that conscious inner struggle had been going on for some time before the conversion.

The most that we need to claim is that Paul had some definite knowledge of Jesus and his gospel before his experience on the Damascus road. The voice that spoke to him out of the light was not the voice of a stranger but rather the voice of a familiar enemy, not one indeed whom he knew at first hand but whose spirit had penetrated the lives of his followers so deeply that to know them was to know him. This is evident in the fact that in the visionary experience Paul hears Jesus saying, "Why do you persecute *me?*" Paul's attempt to destroy the church had been an attempt to complete what was begun in the crucifixion, the silencing of Jesus once and for all in order to remove the threat to existing religion. This establishes a direct continuity between the Jesus of the Gospels and the Christ of Paul. The voice Paul heard was the voice not of a Hellenistic heavenly Lord but of Israel's Lord who had spoken through his prophets in time past and now had spoken decisively and revealed himself decisively in a Son, Jesus of Nazareth. The Christ of the resurrection and the Jesus of the crucifixion are never two entities for

Paul but are indissolubly one, just as they were for the other apostles and as they were to be for the church in its classical creeds.

THE PROBLEM THAT REMAINS

The problem still remains why Paul makes so little reference to anything in Jesus' teaching or in the events of Jesus' ministry to support and corroborate his own teachings and attitudes, particularly since he was attacked in much the same way as Jesus was. When his authority as an apostle was questioned and his gospel was represented as less dependable than what could be heard from the original apostles, he based himself entirely upon Christ's revelation of himself to him as the crucified and risen Lord and insisted that he did not receive either his gospel or his apostleship from any man (Gal. 1:12). It should be noted that this did not exclude the possibility that he had received information concerning Jesus and the Christian movement both before and after his conversion. The Damascus church would not be without traditions concerning Jesus' ministry to which Paul would be exposed as soon as he entered into association there. Then, three years after his conversion he spent fifteen days with Peter in Jerusalem. Is it conceivable that during that time Paul heard nothing from Peter of what he remembered of his association with Jesus in his lifetime? Would Paul have no curiosity, no interest, in knowing what Jesus had said and done before his crucifixion? Some scholars actually portray Paul not just as uninterested in the human story of Jesus but as not *wanting* to know anything about it, since his faith was founded wholly upon the risen Lord. But if it is possible to conceive a Paul with such a strange and inhuman mind-set, which I question, it is certainly not possible to conceive a multitude of Pauline converts and Pauline churches with the same mind-set and completely uninterested in the traditions concerning Jesus that are preserved in the Gospels. Some form of the gospel traditions undoubtedly was present in Paul's churches and was familiar to him. But it was one thing to have knowledge through others concerning Jesus' words and deeds in his lifetime and another to have his gospel from that secondhand knowledge rather than from his immediate confrontation with the risen Lord himself.

Some explanation other than ignorance or disinterestedness must be found for the absence from Paul's letters of references to Jesus' ministry. First, Paul makes very plain that what any church could expect from him was not secondhand knowledge of Jesus' earthly ministry but firsthand knowledge of the gospel as he had received it in direct encounter with Jesus Christ. Since the accusation was made against him that all he knew of Jesus he had learned from the Jerusalem apostles, there would be a natural reticence on his part against basing himself to any degree on information that had come to him from them. All his letters were written after his fifteen-day visit with Peter and after his cooperative relation with Peter in the church at Antioch, yet no trace can be found in them of anything he learned from Peter. Second, he could take for granted the existence in any church to which he wrote of a body of tradition concerning Jesus which was constantly being rehearsed in the services of worship and in the catechetical instruction. A church of Jesus Christ without any traditions concerning Jesus is inconceivable. Third, Paul is an apostle in a sense different from the others. That is immediately evident from the place his writings occupy in the New Testament and the importance he has had for the understanding of the gospel through nineteen centuries. The others, having been with Jesus during his ministry, were custodians of the tradition concerning his words and deeds and, as such, tightly knit together with him in their preaching of his gospel. But Paul, like the author of the Fourth Gospel, is more a reinterpreter of the gospel than a custodian of tradition. If we had transcripts of the preaching of the original disciples, we would likely find in much of it an echoing of the very words and phrases of Jesus. They were in a sense prisoners of Jesus' language while Paul who had never heard Jesus preach or teach was thereby free in his very different situation to find a very different language in which to proclaim the gospel. So different is his language from that of Jesus that he has sometimes been accused of preaching a different gospel. But the more deeply we feel our way behind his language, the more clearly we see that it is the same gospel in a different language for a different situation. Paul had to say it all differently in order to say the same thing. If we compare two prophets such as Amos and Second Isaiah, we see a relation somewhat similar to the relation between Jesus and Paul. They are both servants of the same word of God, concerned both of them to bring their nation before the God who in love had bound them into covenant with himself, from whom alone they could have their one true life, but from the severity of whose judgment there could be no escape except through repentance and forgiveness. But Second Isaiah, while he was bound heart, mind, and soul to the same word of God to which Amos had borne testimony, was not bound at all by Amos' language. His preaching did not have to conform to the preaching of any earlier prophet, but, on the contrary, the immediacy of his relation to the word of God demanded of him an integrity of utterance in his own situation that forbade any mere echoing of a former prophet. Paul's unity with Jesus was at that deeper level, one with him in the gospel which was his very being, his life in God, and therefore free as he went to the Gentile world to say everything in his own way.

The continuity of Paul's gospel with Jesus' gospel is too large a subject to be entered on here, but the salient points can at least be suggested. We have seen how Jesus in his parables and in his controversies with the Pharisees found no cause for pride or self-complacency in any man: all alike were sinners, debtors, sick men in the sight of God. Paul, in the early chapters of Romans, goes to great length in an argumentative fashion to demolish all human complacency, whether Jewish or Gentile, all basis for self-justification, asserting that God has included all in sin that he may have mercy upon all. The heart of the gospel for Paul is the forgiveness of God that is mediated by Jesus Christ: God was in Christ reconciling the world to himself. For Jesus, forgiveness is equally central. He goes seeking men that they may be healed with God's forgiveness and may themselves become mediators of the forgiveness that conquers sin. But when he speaks of this reconciliation, he tells a story of a father welcoming a returning prodigal where Paul develops a doctrinal statement. Paul and Jesus are equally opposed to the idea that any man can make himself right with God by obedience to the law, and where Jesus speaks of a repentance and faith in which a man is utterly humbled and laid open before God, Paul speaks of being justified by faith through grace. Jesus uses the word "justified" only once, when in the parable of the Pharisee and the publican he says of the humbled publican, "This man went down to his house justified." The Kingdom of God in Jesus' gospel has much the same meaning as the righteousness of God in Paul's gospel. One needs to go behind the words "righteousness" and "justification" to their Old Testament usage in order to see this. "Righteousness," "justification" and "salvation" are synonyms in Second Isaiah and in some of the psalms and refer to the new age which will dawn upon the world when God comes to reign openly as sovereign. Also, for both Jesus and Paul the time of salvation, or of the Kingdom, is both present and future. It has come hiddenly, it is coming hiddenly, but one day it will be established openly for all to see. Of course there are radical differences between a Jesus who does not make himself openly the center of his gospel but who nevertheless in his person is central to it and a Paul for whom the whole truth of the gospel is incarnated in Jesus' person, so that to know its truth is to have him take possession of one's very being. But, making allowance for this and for the difference in situation and language, one is impressed by the remarkable unity between the gospel of Jesus and the gospel of Paul and it becomes unbelievable that the risen Lord who encountered Paul on the Damascus road was any other than the Jesus who had been known by Peter and the others in his earthly ministry.

A SUMMING-UP

WHAT, THEN, CAN BE CONCLUDED from these ten studies of the church's memory of Jesus in encounter with representative men? Surely it can be said that the church remembered him as one who set men's present existences radically in question, shattering their complacency about the established religious and social order and provoking severe discomfort, fear, and hatred in some of its pillars. His mission was of a nature to break open the frozen patterns of men's lives and set them moving toward a very different future. But he did this in such a way that the dimensions of the revolution in human life he was generating could, at least for a time, remain concealed even from those who were very close to him. It was a quiet revolution. But it is of the greatest importance for the Christian church and for our whole understanding of the Christian faith that Jesus was a revolutionist.

The two encounters which, if we have interpreted them rightly, make this conclusion inescapable are those with Judas and with Paul. Neither Judas' betrayal of Jesus nor Paul's brutal persecution of the early Christians can be understood except as the reaction of two men who were deeply devoted to their religious heritage to what seemed to them to be a threat to its very existence. The Jesus who is reflected, then, in their encounters with him begins to take on the character of a subverter of the established religious order. The other eight encounters build out the picture, one by one illustrating the sharpness with which

Jesus cut across the lives and the mores of men of his time, some of them representatives of differing streams of religious life in Judaism, some of them members of his own intimate circle. We are better able to understand the original reaction of Paul when we observe how Jesus dealt with Simon the Pharisee or how he answered those who criticized his association with tax collectors. Gradually the picture which emerges is that of a Jesus who in the integrity of his own nature and message constituted a serious affront to the whole accepted order of religion and society in his time, in short a Jesus who was basically committed to a revolution.

Even in Jesus' own time, however, this revolutionary character of his person, his mission, and his message was concealed by the quietness of his approach. It took sharp eyes to see how dangerous he was to the religious institutions of Judaism. He attended the worship of the synagogue. He wore the tasseled prayer shawl. He took delight in the celebration of the traditional Jewish festivals. He made the pilgrimage to Jerusalem for the Passover. He paid his taxes as a law-abiding citizen. He initiated no movements for reform either of the synagogue or the Temple, though he made no secret of his disapproval of elements in both of them. His one public act of protest was against the profanation of the Temple court by commercial interests, but a nation that remembered the prophetic protests of Amos and Jeremiah would surely not be unduly disturbed by such an action. Also, the general character of Jesus' mission had little about it to suggest a revolutionary movement. John the Baptist was puzzled that no dramatic events were taking place. The presence and the coming of the Kingdom was being proclaimed; the sins of men were being forgiven and overcome; people tormented by evil spirits were being liberated, and good news of God was being taken to the poor and the outsiders. Moreover, the mission was largely on the fringe of the Jewish religious community, not in its midst, and there was no evidence that it was capturing any significant support. The number of adherents was very small. It was more annoying than frightening to the authorities, annoying because at so many points Jesus and his followers disregarded the accepted customs, attitudes, and regulations of the religious community. But that warranted only their exclusion, not their persecution.

What accounted for the reaction of Judas and Paul, and of those who became increasingly eager for Jesus' death, was not so much the surface phenomena of Jesus' mission but the growing awareness of a profound contradiction between the order of life that he represented and the order of life that seemed to them to embody all the accumulated values of Israel's religious inheritance. The depth of this contradiction needs to be explored because it is in danger of being concealed anew by some developments of contemporary New Testament scholarship. The investigation of first-century Judaism has turned up a vast amount of material to form a background for the figure of Jesus and has established a great many parallels between his sayings and the sayings of the rabbis. It has been a decided gain to have it emphasized how rooted Jesus was in the Jewish community and the Jewish life of his time. Far too often his first-century Jewishness has been forgotten. But there has been a tendency in some quarters to overdraw the parallels until Jesus becomes only a slightly unusual rabbi of first-century Judaism. Since the Pharisees are recognized validly as the most earnest and devoted representatives of a noble religion and a high ethical standard, it seems impossible that Jesus should have come into such sharp conflict with them, and his severe strictures against them are interpreted as the product of a later age when Christianity and Judaism had become antagonistic rival religions.

What is lacking here is the ability to conceive of a Jesus who would find the most stubborn opponents of his gospel among the earnest, devoted representatives of religion and morality—not just in the first century but in every century since then. It makes no difference that in later ages his opponents have considered themselves to be the spokesmen of a Christian religion and morality. Nothing is more difficult for the average Christian to grasp, even the average Christian scholar, than that a sincerely good religious man may be God's worst enemy, a far more serious obstacle in the way of God's fulfillment of his purpose in history than the worst criminal. This is what makes the assimilation of Jesus to his contemporary Jewish background and the concealment of the contradiction between him and the established order of his day a serious matter for the Christianity of our day. He ceases to be a revolutionary force setting in question the whole order of man's life, not only in the first century but also today. He becomes the incarnation of the higher values of our society, our religion, our morality, rather than the incarnation of the word of God which shakes our world like an earthquake just as it shook the world of first-century Jewish Palestine, and then in the next three centuries the whole Greco-Roman world. The concealment of the contradiction and so of his revolutionary character renders him innocuous and harmless.

Only when the Judaism of Jesus' day is appreciated as the purest and noblest expression of religion in the ancient world can we begin to grasp the significance of the basic revolt that Jesus constituted within it in his person and in his gospel. When Judaism is adequately portrayed, we have to admit that Christian churches have frequently been inferior to it as expressions of religious interest and concern. What began with Jesus can best be understood as permanent revolution, a setting in question of the religious and social order by bringing it under the judgment of God's intention for man, so that as long as the earth shall stand every religious and social order established by men will find itself shaken and laid open to a new future as soon as it lets itself come under that same judging and redeeming word, or perhaps we should say, into that same judging and redeeming presence. The judgment upon the Christian church of today is as severe as it was upon the Judaism of the first century. For us as individuals, or as churches, or as a human society, our confrontation with Jesus strips us of our illusions about our righteousness and of our confidence in the durability of what we have established. We cannot conceive of a time when that will not be so, either for us or for those who come after us. He sets us and our world before God in such a way that we are freed from our inadequate past and set in motion toward the unknown future that God has in store for us.

The depth of the contradiction between Jesus and the men of his time which made him and his gospel a revolutionary force both in Judaism and secondarily in the Greco-Roman world is best understood when he is seen in his context with the Old Testament. In calling his mission the fulfillment of the Old Testament promise he set himself in historical sequence with the prophets and with the purpose of God for all humanity that the prophets had seen unfolding first in Israel. The Kingdom that he heralded was the realm of God's sovereignty, a world restored to God's original intention for it, a humanity truly in covenant with God and reflecting in its relationships his mercy and faithfulness. For Jesus as for the prophets, man constantly stood in a place of decision between two worlds, the world of his own making and the world of God's intention. Man's temptation in every age has been to establish some form of compromise between the two that would let him be at rest, and the call of God has ever been a call to recognize the compromise as a betrayal of God and to launch out afresh toward the hidden goal.

Biblical eschatology is frequently misunderstood as though it were merely a dreaming about the future in which men sought to escape from the distresses and the urgencies of the present. But prophetic eschatology belongs to the essence of the Biblical faith. It brings to expression an impregnable confidence in the ultimate triumph of God's purpose in his creation, an understanding of man's life in history as a journey toward that goal, and a ruthless exposure of the contradiction between the world as it is and the world of God's intention. Man in covenant with God is man in pilgrimage. To be children of God means to sit loose to things as they are so that loyalty to the coming Kingdom transcends every present loyalty. The hope and promise of the future relativizes all the achievements of the past. But at the point where past and future meet, there stands a cross reminding us ever that so wedded are men to the past, especially in their religion, that the journey toward the goal is not always by gentle evolution but at crucial points demands a costly revolution.

But the Jesus who is worshiped and made the object of faith has frequently in our churches been stripped of this revolutionary character so that his gospel has nothing of this prophetic perspective. He no longer is a disturber but before all else provides his worshipers with peace of mind and confidence in their traditional values and religious establishments. It is ironic that the Jesus who was crucified for his refusal to conform to the authoritative religious patterns of his day has so often been made the model and sponsor of the most rigid conformity so that Christians labor under the illusion that they are being loyal to him when they are merely preserving the religious order which is most congenial to themselves. Much of the present-day disillusionment with the church, particularly among its youth, arises from the impression that it is an essentially conservative institution, much more deeply devoted to the *status quo* than to any coming new age.

To the youth, however, who think that devotion to a new age of justice and peace demands of them that they turn their backs on the past and abandon the traditional religious institutions, perhaps even abandon faith in the God who has been worshiped in the past, the Jesus of these encounters may seem to be entirely too gentle and quiet, too patient with his opponents and far too reluctant to seize the power that would have enabled him to hasten the new age. They are impatient with quiet revolutions. They are not interested in a ministry of preaching and teaching, of liberating men from their demons and opening doors for them into the future. But they will do well to consider what issued from the quiet undramatic mission of Jesus. He was not interested in a revolt or reformation that would run its course in a brief generation or less. His concern was for a permanent revolution, and in the few short years of his mission, in his life, death, and resurrection, he laid the foundations of that permanent revolution at such a level that, ever since, each fresh encounter of men with him has become the decisive turning point between the world of the past and God's new age.

NOTES

1. "A Redefinition of Jesus' Use of the Parable," *Expository Times*, Vol. XLVII, No. 12 (September, 1936), p. 551.

2. "Jesus, the Syro-Phoenician Woman, and the Disciples," *Expository Times*, Vol. L, No. 10 (July, 1939), p. 469.

3. R. Travers Herford, *The Pharisees* (The Macmillan Company, 1924).

4. B. Harvie Branscomb, *Jesus and the Law of Moses* (New York, 1930).

5. William Manson, *The Gospel of Luke* (Harper & Brothers, 1930).

6. G. B. Caird, *The Gospel of St. Luke* (Penguin Books, Inc., 1963), p. 114.

7. Joachim Jeremias, *The Parables of Jesus*, tr. by S. H. Hooke (Charles Scribner's Sons, rev. ed., 1955).

8. S. MacLean Gilmour, "Exegesis" in *The Interpreter's Bible*, ed. by George A. Buttrick *et al.*, 12 vols. (Abingdon Press, 1951–1957), Vol. 8, pp. 141–145.

9. Rudolf Bultmann, *The History of the Synoptic Tradition* (Harper & Row, Publishers, Inc., 1963; Göttingen, 1921), p. 21.

10. Alfred Plummer, *The Gospel According to St. Luke*, 5th ed. (International Critical Commentary, Charles Scribner's Sons, 1951), p. 209.

11. Adolf Schlatter, *Die Geschichte des Christus* (1923).

12. K. H. Rengstorf, in *Theologisches Wörterbuch zum Neuen Testament*, ed. by G. Kittel (Stuttgart, 1933 ff.), Vol. I, p. 333.

13. Lucien Cerfaux, *Recueil Lucien Cerfaux* (Gembloux, 1954), Vol. 2.

14. Robert W. Funk, *Language, Hermeneutic, and Word of God* (Harper & Row, Publishers, Inc., 1966).

15. Bultmann, *op. cit.*, p. 51.

16. B. T. D. Smith, *The Parables of the Synoptic Gospels: A Critical Study* (Cambridge: Cambridge University Press, 1937).

17. Gilmour, *loc. cit.*, Vol 8, pp. 195–196.

18. George A. Buttrick, *The Parables of Jesus* (Richard R. Smith, 1930).

19. Adolf Jülicher, *Die Gleichnisreden Jesu* (Leipzig, Vol. I, 1888; Vol. II, 1899).

20. A. T. Cadoux, *The Parables of Jesus: Their Art and Use* (The Macmillan Company, 1931), p. 50.

21. *Ibid.*, p. 59.

22. A. B. Bruce, *Expositor's New Testament* (London, 1900), pp. 217, 216.

23. A. H. McNeile, *The Gospel According to St. Matthew* (London: Macmillan & Company, Ltd., 1915).

24. Erich Klostermann, *Das Matthäusevangelium* (Tübingen: J. C. B. Mohr, 1927).

25. B. Harvie Branscomb, *The Gospel of Mark* (Moffatt New Testament Commentary, Harper & Brothers, 1937).

26. B. H. Streeter, *The Four Gospels: A Study of Origins* (St. Martin's Press, Inc., 1951; London, 1924).

27. J. G. Tasker, "Judas" in *Dictionary of Christ and the Gospels*, ed. by James Hastings, 2 vols. (Charles Scribner's Sons, 1906–1908), Vol. I, p. 907.

28. Jacob S. Golub, *In the Days of the Second Temple* (Cincinnati, 1929).

29. In *Komm Schöpfer Geist* (Munich, 1932), sermons by Karl Barth and Eduard Thurneysen.

30. C. K. Barrett, *The Gospel According to St. John: An Introduction with Commentary and Notes on the Greek Text* (The Seabury Press, Inc., 1958), p. 169.

31. William Wrede, *Paulus* (Tübingen, 1906).